WELSH BORDER
COUNTRY

1 (overleaf) *Llanthony Priory*

MAXWELL FRASER

WELSH BORDER COUNTRY

B. T. Batsford Ltd
London

For

Steve Race

First published 1972

© Maxwell Fraser 1972

Text printed in Great Britain by the Northumberland
Press Ltd, Gateshead, Co. Durham. Plates printed and
books bound by Richard Clay (The Chaucer Press)
Ltd, Bungay, Suffolk for the publishers B. T. Batsford
Ltd, 4 Fitzhardinge Street, London W1

ISBN 0 7134 0072 2

CONTENTS

	List of Illustrations	8
	Map of the Northern Counties	10
	Map of the Southern Counties	12
One	Introduction	15
Two	Chester and the Flintshire Hills	32
Three	St Asaph to Wrexham	50
Four	On the Way to Shrewsbury	67
Five	The Upper Severn Valley	82
Six	The Shropshire Hills	98
Seven	Around Ludlow	116
Eight	The Radnorshire Border	134
Nine	Hereford and the Golden Valley	155
Ten	The Wye Valley	174
Eleven	The Usk Valley	192
	Index	209

LIST OF ILLUSTRATIONS

1. Llanthony Priory — *frontispiece*
2. Fourteenth-century choir stalls, Chester Cathedral — 17
3. Rhuddlan Castle — 18
4. Plowden Hall — 37
5. Hanmer Village — 37
6. Monument to Sir John Wynn, Ruabon Church — 38
7. The White Gates, Leeswood Hall, near Mold — 55
8. Entrance to Chirk Castle — 55
9. Rood screen, Llanwnog Church, near Newtown — 56
10. Fish Street, Shrewsbury — 73
11. Stokesay Castle and Church — 74
12. Monument to Sir John Bridgeman and his wife, Ludlow Church — 91
13 and 14. Sir John Kyrle and his wife, Much Marcle Church — 91
15. Above the Wye Valley, Radnorshire — 92
16. Weobley — 109
17. Staick House, Eardisland — 109
18. The River Wye near Rhayader — 110
19. John Abel's screen, Abbey Dore — 127
20. The River Wye at Hereford — 128
21. Shobdon Church — 145
22. The River Wye at Symonds Yat — 146
23. Kilpeck Church — 163
24. Tudor rood loft, Patrishow Church — 164
25. Exterior of Patrishow Church — 164
26. The River Usk at Crickhowell — 181
27. Llanover Church and the River Usk — 182
28. The Sugar Loaf near Abergavenny — 182
29. The Monnow Gate, Monmouth — 199
30. The River Wye at Chepstow — 200

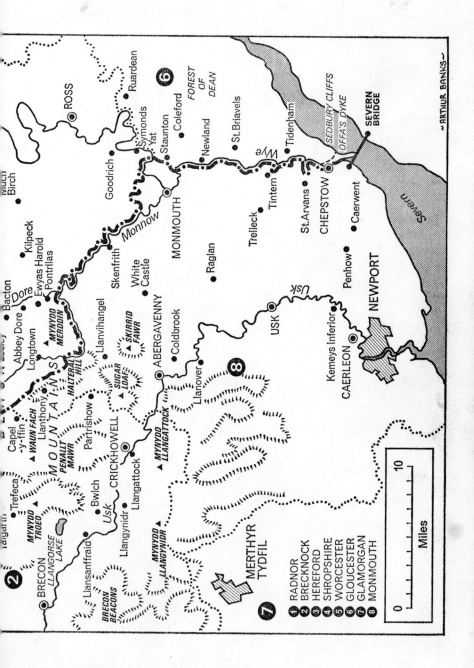

ROSS

Ruardean

6 FOREST OF DEAN

Symonds Yat
Staunton Coleford
Goodrich

Newland St.Briavels

Much Birch

Kilpeck

Monnow

Skenfrith
White Castle

Tintern

Trelleck

St.Arvans CHEPSTOW
Caerwent

SEDBURY CLIFFS
OFFA'S DYKE
Tidenham

SEVERN BRIDGE

Wye

Severn

Bacton
Dore
Ewyas Harold
Abbey Dore Longtown Pontrilas
MYNYDD MERDDIN

Llanvihangel

MONMOUTH

Raglan

Usk

Penhow

NEWPORT

MOUNTAINS
HALTERALL HILL

SKIRRID FAWR

ABERGAVENNY

Coldbrook

USK

Kemeys Inferior

CAERLEON

Capel -y-ffin
WAUN FACH
Llanthony

SUGAR LOAF

Llanover

8

Trefeca
MYNYDD TROED
Partrishow
PENALLT MAWR

CRICKHOWELL

MYNYDD LLANGATTOCK

Tagarth

Bwlch
Llangynidr
Llangattock

MYNYDD LLANGYNIDR

Usk

BRECON
LLANGORSE LAKE

Llansantffraid

MERTHYR TYDFIL

BRECON BEACONS

2

7 ① RADNOR
② BRECKNOCK
③ HEREFORD
④ SHROPSHIRE
⑤ WORCESTER
⑥ GLOUCESTER
⑦ GLAMORGAN
⑧ MONMOUTH

0   10

Miles

~ARTHUR BANKS~

CHAPTER ONE

Introduction

The traveller approaching the Welsh Border from England sees the hills and mountains of Wales rising like a wall along the eastern edge of the English Midland Plain. Only in south Shropshire are there hills thrusting out into England, around Ludlow and Church Stretton.

On closer acquaintance, the barrier is seen to be broken into many different ranges and high plateaux, penetrated by innumerable river valleys, but this first impression of the contrast between the Pre-Cambrian uplands and the newer rocks of the English lowlands, makes it easier to understand how the Welsh maintained their independence for so many centuries against successive invasions by Romans, Anglo-Saxons and Normans.

The only parts of the Border where industry has penetrated are in Flintshire, Monmouthshire and Denbighshire. In Flintshire, all the great industries are crowded into the narrow strip of level ground beside the Dee estuary, leaving the far greater area of the upland region untouched.

Monmouthshire rejoices in two of the loveliest and most romantic river valleys of the Border—the lower Wye and the Usk—which are separated from the industrial valleys by barriers of mountains. Nor are the industrial regions of Monmouthshire so devoid of charm as those who do not know them imagine. I lived in Monmouthshire, on a high ridge above two mining valleys, with great hills on every side, and could step out into a field sloping steeply to a wooded dingle where bluebells, primroses, violets, honeysuckle, dog roses, and even wild strawberries and raspberries grew in profusion, and the only sounds were the plashing of a crystal-clear brook, the song of the birds, and the rustle of wild animals in the undergrowth.

Only between Wrexham and Ruabon, in the neck of Denbighshire thrusting east to the Cheshire boundary, is modern industrialization inescapable, making an unsightly approach to the lovely Vale of Llangollen, but even here it is a matter of only a few miles to more attractive scenery.

Many a poet and novelist born on this borderland has shed light on some facet of history, legend, or everyday life there, but as yet no writer has fused its traditions into poetry and prose which is the cultural heritage of all England, as well as of the Welsh Border, as Scott did for the Scottish Border. This must surely be due to the extreme length and diversity of the Welsh Border, and to the rival claims of the Welsh and English languages, rather than to any lack of material, for this borderland is unique in Britain for the multiplicity of its defensive works and the variety of its scenery. Iron Age camps, Roman forts, Anglo-Saxon dykes, Norman mottes and medieval castles cluster more thickly than anywhere else in Great Britain. The stone castles range from fragments which are now scarcely identifiable to Powis and Chirk, which have been inhabited continuously to the present day. They bear witness to a troubled history of over 1,500 years, and to events which have changed the course of history in England, as well as in Wales.

The Prehistory of the Border was the Prehistory of Britain, for the Celtic chieftains of the Iron Age, and the Bronze Age men they conquered, inhabited the whole of the country as far north as Strathclyde. The first demarcation line was drawn by the Romans, with their road between Deva (Chester) and Isca (Caereon), marking the boundary between the Romanized Britons of the plain, and the semi-independent Britons of the mountainous regions.

The Romans overcame the Deceangli of North Wales with comparative ease but the Ordovices of Mid-Wales and the Silures of South Wales fought with desperate courage, and held out until some time after A.D. 50 under their brave leader Caradog (Caractacus). It is a measure of his fame that so many hills not only on the Welsh side of the Border, but in the Shropshire hill country, are named after him, and claim to be the scene of his last stand before he was defeated and sent captive to Rome.

2 *Fourteenth-century choir stalls, Chester Cathedral*

When the last of the legions left Britain, early in the fifth century, Saxon invasions began in earnest. It was the fierce resistance of the Britons which gave rise to the Arthurian legends, on which some of the greatest literature of Western Europe has been based—legends so confused that all it is possible to claim is that they had some historical basis, however slight, but of such perennial interest to scholars all over the world that an International Arthurian Congress was held in 1931 to enable Arthurian scholars to have an opportunity for an exchange of views. Another Congress was held in 1948, and an International Arthurian Society was founded which now holds a Congress every three years.

It was in the Welsh Border that Geoffrey of Monmouth wrote his *Historia Regum Britanniae*; and although no place can be identified unquestionably as the scene of Arthur's exploits, Caereon is associated with Arthur's Court, in name at least, and Knucklas, on the Radnorshire-Breconshire boundary, is said to have been the home of Guinevere.

The Britons won for themselves 50 years of peace in the first half of the sixth century, during which literature flourished, the tribal territories of Wales became kingdoms, and Celtic monks travelled far and wide in the Celtic countries and the Border. This was the 'Age of Saints', when Celtic missionaries founded hundreds of churches bearing their names. Many of the sites can be identified all over Wales and across the Border, particularly in south Herefordshire.

The Celtic Church had a completely different organization from that of the Church of Rome, and its bishops exercised a purely spiritual function, with no territorial jurisdiction, and the Saints were men of great simplicity of life. They did not feel the urge to build impressive churches, and in later centuries, wherever the Normans occupied the land, they replaced the little wattle and daub churches with stone buildings. They disregarded the Celtic saints, who had never been canonized by the Roman Church, and rededicated them to the saints they themselves reverenced. The modest Saxon churches, although frequently of stone, fared no better, and Saxon saints were mostly discarded. In the course of time, too, place-names on both sides of the Border became so corrupted that the philologist who tries to trace their origins treads a more than usually perilous path.

It was in this period that the Britons who were separated from their kinsmen in Strathclyde and Cornwall by the advancing Saxons began to call themselves 'Cymry' (fellow countrymen), and were known by the Saxons as 'Wealas' (Welshmen) or strangers.

The Anglo-Saxon Chronicle, which records the principal events of the invasion of Britain from the landing of Hengist and Horsa in A.D. 449 until the Norman Conquest, is complemented by *Brut y Tywysogion* (Chronicle of the Princes) embodying the Welsh point of view, from A.D. 681 to 1332.

The battles of Chester in A.D. 615 and Oswestry in 641 brought the Anglo-Saxons to their most westerly point along the north and central borderland, with the Wye marking the southern limit of the Kingdom of Mercia. King Penda of Mercia achieved the unification of the Angles and Saxons on the Welsh Border, but the Mercians in their turn were conquered by the West Saxons in A.D. 889. The Saxons never succeeded in penetrating permanently any farther into Wales, and the great dyke built by King Offa of Mercia in the eighth century was as much an admission of this failure, as a boundary line and defence against the Welsh.

The line of Offa's Dyke is a few miles west of the earlier Wat's Dyke, which ran south from Basingwerk in Flintshire to the Morda Brook in Shropshire. Offa's Dyke runs from the north coast near Prestatyn to the Sedbury Cliffs above the Severn estuary. Many miles can be traced in an unbroken line over hill and dale in the central portion, with shorter sections in the north and south in various stages of preservation. There are also some short dykes of an earlier date, chiefly in Herefordshire.

The Offa's Dyke Path was designated in 1955 as one of six national footpaths planned in Britain, but comparatively little progress was made until The Offa's Dyke Association (Cymdeithas Clawdd Offa), formed in 1969, blazed a trail, and the work was taken up by local authorities on the route, who erected stiles and signposts and negotiated rights of way. The Path was opened officially in 1971 by Lord Hunt, a native of Knighton, Radnorshire, which is right on the line of the Dyke.

The Association has mapped the Offa's Dyke Path, which is 168 miles in length. It follows the Dyke for most of the way, deviating only where some special feature or view can be included. The extremely readable Shell Guide *The Offa's Dyke Path* by Frank Noble, founder and honorary secretary of the Association, gives detailed instructions and advice, and dedicated archaeologists can consult *Offa's Dyke* by Sir Cyril Fox. The Offa's Dyke Path is certainly one of the finest footpaths in Britain, offering a succession of marvellous panoramic views, historical associations, access to some of the most sparsely inhabited districts on the Border, opportunities for observing wild life, and accommodation in delightful little villages or market towns.

The Saxons had little cultural or ethnic influence on the Welsh, but the Normans were a very different matter. When William the Conqueror had subdued the Saxons of England, he dealt with the constant menace of the war-like Welsh by creating the March (Mark, or boundary). Choosing the most rapacious and unruly of his Norman followers, who might otherwise have menaced his own authority, he created the Marcher Earldoms of Hereford, Shrewsbury and Chester, and gave to them and numerous lesser lords leave to keep any lands they could wrest from the Welsh, and to rule their conquered possessions as absolute despots.

On the eve of the Norman Conquest of England, the unification of the numerous smaller kingdoms of Wales which had begun in the ninth century had seen the emergence of the four large kingdoms of Gwynedd, on the north-west; Powys on the north-east; Deheubarth on the south-west; and Morgannwg on the south, each of which was divided into cantrefs or hundreds. Although the size and power of these kingdoms fluctuated, their princes remained the chief leaders against the English until the Statute of Rhuddlan in 1284.

The complex story of the rise and fall of the Welsh dynasties, and the advance of the Norman lords, can be found in enthralling detail in Sir John Lloyd's *History of Wales from the earliest times to the Edwardian Conquest*. Only a brief account of the chief protagonists can be given here.

When Bleddyn ap Cynfyn, who had succeeded in making himself king of Gwynedd as well as of Powys, died in 1075, none of his sons was old enough to succeed him. Gruffydd ap Cynan made himself ruler of Gwynedd, and gradually extended his power until first William Rufus, and later Henry I, led fruitless expeditions against him. Although his lifetime coincided with the fiercest Norman attacks on Wales, when he died in 1137 at the age of 82 he was undisputed ruler of a kingdom extending from Anglesey to the Vale of Clwyd and south to the borders of Deheubarth.

Gruffydd's eldest son, Owain, succeeded him, and in order to distinguish him from his rival Owain ap Gruffydd of the royal line of Powys, he became known as Owain Gwynned, and the latter as Owain Cyfeiliog. It was during Owain Gwynedd's reign that the titles of 'king' and 'prince' were dropped by Welsh rulers for the less provocative title of 'lord'. Only the rulers of Gwynedd retained the title of 'prince', apparently by general agreement about 1154. This was another period of great national revival, during which one of the greatest Welsh poems of the twelfth century was written by Gwalchmai, in praise of Owain Gwynedd. It has been translated into English by Thomas Gray, under the title of *The Triumphs of Owen*.

In South Wales, Rhys ap Tewdwr, the last completely independent ruler of Deheubarth, was killed by the Normans in Brecheiniog (Breconshire) in 1093, and his son, Gruffydd, after several unsuccessful attempts to regain his ancestral lands, made his peace with Henry I. He died in 1137. The most famous of his four sons was Rhys ap Gruffydd, always known as Yr Arglwydd Rhys (The Lord Rhys), who met and made friends with Henry II, and was officially recognized as ruler of Deheubarth.

On the death of The Lord Rhys in 1197, the leading role fell again to the royal line of Powys, which had achieved prominence under Madog ap Maredudd, who is described in the *Mabinogion*, in *The Dream of Rhonabwy*, as undisputed lord of Dudleston and all the land between Ceiriog and the Vyrnwy. He was succeeded by his nephew, Owain Cyfeiliog, who, unlike Owain Gwynedd, was almost always in alliance with the English. He consolidated the prosperity of Powys, but is best remembered as a gifted poet. His surviving poems shed considerable light on the life of the people of Powys under his rule. He died in 1197, and was buried at Ystrad Marchell

(*Strata Marcella*), the Cistercian Abbey he had founded. He was succeeded by the headstrong Gwenwynwyn, who figures in Scott's novel, *The Betrothed*. After some early successes he was so decisively defeated by Llywelyn Fawr (the Great) that the leadership passed again to the Prince of Gwynedd. Llywelyn ab Iorwerth (Llywelyn Fawr), born in 1173, ruled over a united Wales until his death in 1240. Dafydd ap Llywelyn failed to consolidate the work of his father, but Llywelyn's grandson, Llywelyn ap Gruffydd, who succeeded in 1246, set himself to assume supreme power. By 1267, he had acquired wider lands and a greater authority than any Welsh prince had wielded since the Norman Conquest, only to be finally defeated by Edward I. Although his statesmanship had proved unsuccessful—largely because he alienated the other Welsh leaders by his ambition—he was deeply mourned as the last native Prince and champion of Wales, and to many his death meant the end of all things. The bard Gruffydd ab yr Ynad Coch summed up the national feeling: 'Great torrents of wind and rain shake the whole land, the oak trees clash together in a wild fury, the sun is dark in the sky and the stars have fallen from their courses'.

Even allowing for their human failings, and the natural exaggeration of the bards singing their praises, the leaders who successively united Wales, in the face of Norman pressure, must have been remarkable men, especially when it is remembered that at no time before 1500 did the population of Wales exceed a quarter of a million, whilst the population of England had reached two million as early as the twelfth century.

It was the memory of these heroic princes which kept alive the national spirit long after all hope seemed to have fled, and led to the revolt under Owain Glyn Dŵr.

Much has been written both for and against Owain Glyn Dŵr, but more is now known of the background of the revolt, enabling a fresh assessment to be made. As Professor Glanmor Williams points out, the century or so which followed the Edwardian conquest of Wales was a time of great difficulty and distress all over Europe, and the king's officials in Wales and the March grew ever more oppressive in their demands. Welshmen were longing for a leader to throw off the foreign yoke. Glyn Dŵr's success was so immediate and so complete, and so invariably aided by that greatest ally of the Welsh in their wars, the weather, that the English credited him with magical powers.

He chose some of the most able men of the time as his bishops and advisers and, had he been able to maintain the independence of Wales, it would have had its own Church and University centuries earlier. In 1407 his luck deserted him, and by 1412 he was a fugitive and an outlaw—but it is to be noted that no one ever betrayed him. He disappeared so completely that it is unknown when or where he died and was buried.

The immediate consequences were catastrophic. Savage penal laws were passed by the English Parliament against the Welsh. Large areas of Wales had been ravaged, and it is one of the charges against him that he destroyed abbeys and churches of great antiquarian interest. Admittedly he waged war in the fashion of his age, and had personal ambitions, but there must have been something over and above this to inspire such devotion. He fought for an ideal of independence shared by many, if not all of his fellow countrymen, and these ideals remained. He did for Wales what William Wallace and Robert the Bruce did for Scotland and Joan of Arc for France; he gave them an awareness of national identity. As Professor Trevelyan says, he was 'an attractive and unique figure in a period of debased and selfish politics', and he inspired his countrymen to survive as a nation in the face of every adversity.

The first Norman assault on Wales was led by William Fitzosbern, a kinsman of William the Conqueror, who was created Earl of Hereford in 1067. He built a series of frontier posts as he advanced into Wales. His earliest motte and bailey castles were at Wigmore, Ewyas Harold and Clifford-on-Wye, on Saxon land. They were followed by Striguil (Chepstow), the first Norman castle built on Welsh soil, and Monmouth. He died in 1071, and his son Roger, who rebelled against the king, was imprisoned for life. No new earl was created, and the attack on South Wales was left to the Mortimers, Toesnis, Lacys, FitzBalderuns and Says, the lords of Cleobury, Clifford, Ludlow, Monmouth and Clun, with the de Clares at Striguil.

Roger of Montgomery, created Earl of Shrewsbury in 1070, led the assault on Powys, and built a castle at Montgomery, but the third Earl forfeited his earldom in 1102 by persistent treason against Henry 1. Here, again, no new earl was created, and further advances were left to the Braoses of Radnor, Corbets of Caus, Fitzalans of Oswestry, and Lacys of Ewyas (Longtown).

The history of the conquest of North Wales followed a different course. The Saxon Earl Edwin, having submitted to the Conqueror, was left in possession of the earldom of Chester, but following his rebellion, the earldom was bestowed on a Norman who made so little headway against the Welsh that William 1 bestowed the earldom on his nephew, Hugh Lupus (the Wolf) of Avranches, who dominated the advance into North Wales for 30 years, ably assisted by his chief lieutenant, Robert of Rhuddlan, who was as cruel and ruthless as his lord.

The pattern of the leading Marcher families of the earlier conquests, who established the triple line of defences along the Border, changed constantly in later periods as families died out in the male line and heiresses married into other families, or lands were confiscated by the English king. Of the 136 Marcher lordships mentioned in the Act of Union, 41 had become Crown lordships either by conquest, forfeiture or marriage.

In the zone of some 30 to 50 miles deep which they had conquered, the Normans introduced their own laws and culture, as alien to the Saxons as to the Welsh. In some areas, Welsh communities which had submitted to Norman overlordship were left free to live by their ancient laws and customs, but as a rule Normans, Saxons and Welsh were fused together in varying combinations and degrees to produce the sturdy Border types of today.

Large-scale farming was introduced, towns founded, and trade organized on a scale never before attempted by the pastoral communities of the Border, and the ancient Celtic Church was reorganized on territorial and diocesan lines, to bring it under the rule of Canterbury, and integrate it with the Church of Western Christendom.

Although the Celtic Church had remained orthodox on the vital matter of doctrine, it had divergent practices which had grown up during the long separation from Rome, and the Celtic clergy fought stubbornly to retain them. It was not until 1138 that the last Celtic usage, that of married clergy, was abolished finally and, in spite of continual pressure, the Welsh Church did not submit completely to Canterbury until Giraldus Cambrensis finally lost his magnificent fight for its complete freedom. It was over 700 years before it shook off the dominance of Canterbury, and became the Church of Wales.

Giraldus Cambrensis (Gerallt Cymro: Gerald the Welshman), as Archdeacon of Brecon, was closely associated with the Border. He is as famous in English as in Welsh literature for his Itineraries through Wales and Ireland, and *Description of Wales*. His lively curiosity and racy style make them delightful reading, and his shrewd comments on local conditions, in spite of his tinge of medieval credulity, make them invaluable sources of information about everyday life in Wales and Ireland in the twelfth century.

He was one of the numerous grandchildren of the powerful Norman lord, Gerald de Windsor, and his wife, the Welsh Princess Nest, and was related to the Geraldines of Ireland. His *Autobiography* reveals his pride in his descent, his love of his childhood home in Manorbier Castle, and the details of his strenuous and long-drawn-out but ill-fated struggle to gain confirmation of his election as Bishop of St David's, and to free the Welsh Church from the domination of Canterbury, which ended in 1203 when the Prior of Llanthony was appointed Bishop of St David's. Giraldus devoted the remaining 23 years of his life to literature.

Although the Normans were completely successful in the lowlands and valleys, they never succeeded in conquering the Welsh in the more mountainous regions. There is still a marked difference between the size and magnificence of some of the churches in the eastern counties of Wales, where the Norman style of architecture spills over the Border, and the simpler churches of the western counties.

When Edward I conquered Wales and created his eldest son the first English Prince of Wales, he took over the lands of Llewelyn the Last, but left the Marcher Lords undisturbed. Many Welsh soldiers followed the English kings to the wars in France and Scotland. When the Black Prince was unhorsed at Crécy, it was the flag with the Red Dragon of Cadwaladr, a seventh-century Welsh hero, and the recognized emblem of the Welsh, which was flung over him in protection until his enemies were beaten off. Nor must it be forgotten that the famous 'English' long-bow originated in Wales, and was first used by the men of Gwent, Morgannwg and Brecheiniog against the Angevins. Edward I was the first English king to realize the superiority of the long-bow over the cross-bow. The earliest full account of the scientific use of the long-bow is at Falkirk in 1298, where the greater number of Edward's bowmen were Welsh. It was the combined use of long-bowmen and cavalry which gave the English kings their great series of victories, and made them the fear and wonder of their time.

Tretower Court, then a seat of the Vaughans, was a rallying point for the Welsh archers who fought at Agincourt, and those who know Shakespeare's *Henry V* will remember that the king was proud to have been born a Welshman at Monmouth, and that Sir David Gam, a Breconshire man, was one of those killed in the battle.

Trouble broke out again on the Border—and, indeed, all over England and Wales—during the Wars of the Roses. The Mortimers were deeply involved on the Yorkist side, and Edmund Mortimer joined Owain Glyn Dŵr in his revolt, which lasted from 1400 to 1415.

It was not until the reign of Edward IV that any real attempt was made to restrict the powers of the Lords Marcher, and deal with the increasing lawlessness of fugitives from royal justice who found refuge in the March.

The Council of the Marches of Wales was instituted in 1471, and although it was not always effective under the weaker Presidents, it brought some measure of relief. Much was done under the presidency of Roland Lee, Bishop of Coventry and Lichfield, who was appointed Lord President of the Council in 1535, and retained the office until his death in 1543, but it was not until 1536, when the Marcher lordships were abolished finally, that peace came to the Border. People living in the Marches, instead of being tenants subject to private lords exercising the powers of life and death over them, became subject to the king's courts. The Marcher lordships were merged into counties, and the five new counties of Denbigh, Montgomery, Radnor, Brecon and Monmouth were created. The Council of the Marches of Wales was continued as a convenient administrative body, but was finally abolished in 1689.

27

After the accession of the Tudor King, Henry VII, all the richer and more influential gentry of Wales had flocked to the Court in London, and after the Acts of Union, many followed the lead of Henry VIII, who was determined to see the two nations completely integrated. English was the official language of the administration, and no one could hold office who did not speak it, but no actual attempt was made to forbid the use of the Welsh tongue, and two events on the Border ensured the survival of the language.

During the reign of Elizabeth I, an eisteddfod was held at Caerwys in Flintshire, to regulate the bardic organization, and weed out the impostors from the genuine poets; and the Bible was translated into Welsh by Bishop Morgan, then Rector of Llanrhaeadr-ym-Mochnant in Montgomeryshire. The new Welsh Bible not only standardized Welsh prose, but is regarded as having been the greatest unifying force in the Welsh national consciousness. The Welsh language persisted, and even along the Border it was still spoken until at least the mid-nineteenth century, as is shown in George Borrow's *Wild Wales*.

Today, Radnorshire has been entirely Anglicized, and the other Welsh Border counties have only a minority speaking Welsh. This may well change in the future, as Welsh is now being taught in many schools on the Welsh side of the Border, particularly in Flintshire.

It was in the Tudor period that the English and Welsh sides of the Border became more closely integrated through the rising tide of prosperity. The Welsh woollen industry, which dates back to the earliest times, increased greatly, particularly in Montgomeryshire, for which Shrewsbury was the chief market, and flourished until a setback during the Napoleonic wars, and its final decline through the rise of the Australian wool trade.

Droving also increased in importance. Welsh drovers moved along the old drovers' roads to the rich markets of Chester, Shrewsbury and Hereford, and even to London. All the roads can be traced today, and some of them have been metalled to take motor traffic through their spectacular scenery. There are many place-names and inn signs to perpetuate the memory of the drovers, and there were even special drovers' banks, for the drovers became men of substance, entrusted by the gentry with financial operations. Droving remained a prosperous trade until the coming of the railways.

Few places in Britain benefited more than the borderland from the improvement in the economy and in living conditions during the Tudor period. Most of the domestic buildings of the Border were built by the newly prosperous merchants. Castles abandoned by the leading families for more spacious and comfortable mansions proved a rich quarry for building materials, and for the first time the poor cottagers were able to have reasonably habitable and permanent cottages—now one of the joys of the Border in their picturesqueness. It must have given them a fierce joy to despoil the castles of their former oppressors.

The mellow timber-framed, red-brick houses of Herefordshire and the black and white 'magpie' houses of Herefordshire, Shropshire and Cheshire are also found in some of the Welsh Border towns, and here, too, are the most beautiful churches in Wales, usually small, but filled with extraordinarily rich woodwork, and stained glass, dating chiefly from the fifteenth and sixteenth centuries.

During the seventeenth and eighteenth centuries, many people from both sides of the Border emigrated to the Americas to seek religious freedom, and there was disruption during the Civil War period, but this was balanced by the Industrial Revolution in the nineteenth century, which attracted even larger numbers of immigrants from England and Ireland. Unfortunately the new developments also drew men of the Border from the agricultural districts, and many a farm and cottage was left to fall into ruin. The greatest depopulation was in Herefordshire and Central Wales. Those who see the richness of the Herefordshire soil, and know the fame of its pedigree cattle, must find it hard to realize that its population is declining steadily. A quarter of the county's 127,000 people live in Hereford, and large areas have been afforested since 1945. In Central Wales the depopulation has continued to such an extent that a Mid-Wales Development Council was set up in 1968 to devise a means of combating it. Among other plans, an enlargement of Newtown is envisaged which would link it up with Caersws, higher up the Severn valley.

The depopulation which is so tragic to the people affected, especially those dispossessed by the creation of large reservoirs of water to serve the English Midlands, and the ever-increasing afforestation, lends the countryside additional charm to the eyes of the visitor. It is doubtful if the Montgomeryshire hill country will be affected by the development plans—after all, is it not an article of faith with anyone born in Montgomeryshire that it is *'Powys Paradwys Cymru'* (Powys the Paradise of Wales)? The natural beauty of the Border has also been safeguarded by the creation of the Brecon Beacons National Park, with three special Nature Reserves, and by the designation of the Forest of Dean as a National Forest Park, and there is the possibility of more areas being added in the future to link the Brecon Beacons National Park with the Snowdonia National Park.

No two writers on the Welsh Border Country have agreed on its exact area, but to me it seems logical to follow the routes of the Lords Marcher who created the Marcher country. Inevitably, in covering such a wide area, many places of great interest must be omitted, and to those who find no mention of some beloved haunt, I can say only that I regret having to leave out so much, including some of my own favourite places—but this should add zest to travel in the region, by leaving visitors the possibility of making 'discoveries' of their own.

It cannot be stressed too strongly that the ideal way to explore the Border country is on foot or on horseback, but few people nowadays can spare enough time for a leisurely exploration covering so many miles. Some hardy souls attempt it with a bicycle, which is comparatively easy in the English counties or the wider Welsh valleys—although even here, there are very few level stretches in the undulating countryside, and not a few surprisingly steep hills—but it can be exhausting in the extreme on Welsh hill ranges, which are seldom under 1,000 feet, and often over 2,000 feet in height, and intimidatingly steep into the bargain.

Although some of the ancient trackways over the hills are now metalled and possible for motor-cars, others can be impassable in bad weather, and all are dangerous when the heights are enveloped in mist. On the footpaths, particularly in the Berwyns, there is the added peril of peat bogs.

Seeing the Border on a sunny day in winter, with the delicate tracery of the bare tree branches etched against the snow, it is hard to realize that snow can be a deadly hazard on the hill ranges. On a glorious spring morning, when the trees are bursting into leaf, and the orchards are covered in blossom; or a hot summer day, when the air is fragrant with the heady scent of gorse and honeysuckle; or an autumnal day when bracken and trees flame russet and gold, it is still less easy to realize that there can be a sudden downpour of rain as devastating as in the days when whole armies were put to rout by the weather alone. It is well to keep in mind the experience of Henry IV on his expedition against Owain Glyn Dŵr in 1402. The king 'pitched his tents in a very pleasant meadow where everything seemed to betoken a calm and comfortable night', only to be struck by floods of rain followed by a whirlwind, which compelled the king and his army to return 'bootless and weather-beaten back'.

Luckily such intemperate weather is infrequent, and with the great increase in motoring holidays, the visitor with limited time can move from one centre to another by car, and explore the neighbourhood of each on foot, or with one of the pony-trekking clubs. I have explored all parts of the Border on foot, but still find an unending exhilaration from the breathtaking panoramic views on a car ride across Llangynidr Mountain, Clun Forest, Wenlock Edge, the Berwyns, or the hills of Flintshire above the estuary of the Dee—to name but a few out of so many memorable roads of the Border.

There is also an ever-diminishing service of buses, a railway line from Chester to Newport, and the Central Wales line from Swansea to Craven Arms.

CHAPTER TWO

Chester and the Flintshire Hills

Although unmistakably an English town, Chester's early history was bound up with that of Wales. It was the headquarters for expeditions against the Welsh for over a thousand years. The fifteenth-century Welsh bard, Lewis Glyn Cothi, had good reason to abuse the city in his poetry—although it must be admitted he had a personal grudge against its citizens to inflame his patriotism.

Chester is the only completely walled city surviving in England, with wide, straight streets following the lines laid down by the Roman engineers, and bordered by the famous 'Rows'. Fuller, writing in the first half of the seventeenth century, described the Rows as:

> ...galleries wherein passengers go dry without coming into the streets, having shops on both sides and underneath, the fashion whereof is somewhat hard to conceive. It is therefore worth their pains, who have money and leisure, to make their own eyes the expounders of the manner thereof....

There are now shops on one side of the galleries only, but the shops at street level remain.

Even those most opposed to the replacement of ancient buildings by modern replicas, must surely admit that at Chester the mingling of many genuinely ancient houses, each with some special architectural feature or historic interest, with good examples of Victorian black and white buildings, has been done with discretion. It has preserved a remarkable picture of Tudor and Stuart street frontages, and the city centre is too alive with traffic and shoppers to be a 'museum' piece.

Chester also has some very attractive eighteenth-century town houses of Cheshire county families, or the homes of wealthy merchants. Outside the city walls there is an ever-growing rash of modern building, most of it abysmally dull, but with occasional flashes of genuine inspiration.

If the old houses of Chester are a testimony to the wealth and taste of its citizens, the number and magnificence of its surviving churches is a testimony to their piety, which has not always been respected by their descendants. The medieval Chapel of St Nicholas has had a very chequered career—in turn a theatre, where Grimaldi, Garrick, Kean, John Kemble and Mrs Siddons acted; a music hall, in which Charles Dickens gave a reading in 1867; a cinema; and now a supermarket.

After exploring the busy streets, and walking the two miles of city walls, it is refreshing to sit in the quiet, sunny garden of the cathedral cloisters. The exterior of the cathedral looks disappointingly new, but those who have read the dismal accounts of its crumbling fabric, before the restoration in the nineteenth century, must be thankful it has been so carefully preserved. The interior is full of treasures. The fourteenth-century choir stalls, with their canopies and misericords, are superbly carved, and the monastic buildings are unusually complete. The thirteenth-century refectory, with an elaborate stone pulpit where a monk read to the brethren during meals, has a splendid modern hammerbeam roof, designed by F. H. Crossley of Chester, which shows that the ancient craft of woodworking has by no means been lost. The Chester Imp, which figures on so many of the souvenirs sold in the city, can be seen in the nave.

Chester was founded by the Romans, who built Deva in a loop of the River Dee, and it was garrisoned for 300 years by the 20th Legion, the *Valeria Victrix*. Nearly 13,000 men were stationed there. The foundations of their barracks, baths, military hospital and burial ground, and the amphitheatre where they relieved the boredom of garrison duty, can be seen in the cellars of some of the shops in the Rows, or just outside the city walls. There is a comprehensive collection of models, plans and carvings in the Grosvenor Museum.

Famous names light up the Saxon era in Chester—the seventh-century St Werburg, to whom the cathedral is dedicated, daughter of Merewald, the first Christian King of Mercia; Æthelflaed, the redoubtable daughter of King Alfred; King Edgar, the first Saxon to be crowned King of a united England; St Dunstan, who crowned him; and Earl Leofric and his wife, the famous Lady Godiva.

William the Conqueror visited Chester in 1069, and the following year Hugh, Earl of Chester, was made a Count Palatine. Cheshire was the first County Palatine, or Royal County, an honour it enjoys in the present day, when H.R.H. Prince Charles is not only Prince of Wales but also Earl of Chester.

Many English kings and queens visited Chester in triumph—and sometimes in disaster. Richard II held the city in the highest esteem, and his personal bodyguard of 2,000 archers was drawn largely, if not entirely, from Cheshire, which must have made the contrast all the more bitter, when he and the Earl of Salisbury were brought as prisoners to Chester Castle, riding through the streets on what were described contemptuously as 'two little nagges not worth 40 francs'. Scarcely less bitter was the departure of Charles I, after watching from the city walls the defeat of his troops at Rowton Moor in September 1645. He left the stout-hearted Cestrians to continue their defence, and cover his retreat, although they must have known his cause was lost.

During the thirteenth and early fourteenth centuries, Chester was the most important port in the north-west, trading with Ireland, Scotland, Spain and the Low Countries. This, too, was the time when the Chester Nativity plays were written by monks of Chester. Archdeacon Rogers, who saw the plays in 1594, says:

The manner of these plays were, every company had his pageant or part, a high scaffold with two rooms, a higher and a lower, upon four wheels. In the lower they apparelled themselves, and in the higher room they played, being all open on the top that all beholders might hear and see them.... They began first at the abbey gates, and when the first pageant was played, it was wheeled to the high cross before the mayor, and so to every street. So every street had a pageant playing before it at one time till all the pageants for the day appointed were played. When one pageant was near ended, word was brought from street to street, that so they might come in place thereof, exceeding orderly, and all the streets have their pageants before them, all at one time playing together; to see which plays was great resort and also scaffolds and stages made in the streets in those places where they determined to play their pageants.

The plays were given during the first three days of Whitsuntide, and were divided into 24 pageants, according to the number of the City Companies. One of the Chester Plays furnished the libretto for Benjamin Britten's *Noyes Fludde*.

By the fifteenth century, the silting up of the Dee estuary had begun to interfere with traffic to the harbour. Despite desperate attempts by the city authorities to keep the channel clear, and build a new port farther along the estuary, the sea-borne trade of Chester was gradually transferred to the then obscure little fishing village of Liverpool. The only reminder of Chester's maritime greatness today is the proud title of 'Admiral of the Dee' assumed by each Mayor of Chester by virtue of his office, although the head of the estuary is now five miles from the city walls. It says much for the tenacity of the Cestrians that after a period of great difficulty, they succeeded in building up an inland trade, and regained their prosperity.

Those who have travelled along the Flintshire shore of the Dee estuary in an over-crowded train, or been caught in one of those 12-mile traffic jams which are all too frequent there during holiday weekends, will find it difficult to believe that Flintshire (Sir Fflint) is a delightful, but almost entirely neglected county, so far as the inland districts are concerned.

There are huge factories and council estates in the narrow strip of land between the estuary and the low, rather dusty-looking line of hills, and there are vast caravan sites along the North Wales coast, but the far larger inland region of hills, small streams, and woodlands is unknown to all but a few who love it.

Leaving Chester by the Hawarden (pronounced 'Harden') road (A.55), the boundary between England and Wales is crossed at Saltney, which has grown until it is inextricably mixed with the suburbs of Chester. It will not detain anyone in search of beauty. Soon, the road mounts a little and skirts a great park, before entering the main street of Hawarden (Penarlag) which is sufficiently wide to accommodate modern traffic comfortably. Although there are few buildings of any age surviving, Hawarden's houses contrive to make up an attractive whole. An eye should be kept open for the 'House of Correction' on the right. The mellow stone-work is so beautifully proportioned that it is a delight to the eye, although this can have given little consolation to anyone incarcerated in its restricted and comfortless interior. It is now scheduled as an Ancient Monument.

After the construction of Offa's Dyke, Hawarden found itself a part of the Kingdom of Mercia, although it was again in the hands of the Welsh in the tenth century. At the Norman Conquest it came under the overlordship of Hugh Lupus, Earl of Chester, and is mentioned in Domesday Book as the chief manor and capital of the Hundred of Alticross, which extended from the Dee to the Vale of Clwyd. The rest of Alticross changed hands many times, but Hawarden never again came under Welsh rule, except for a few short years in the thirteenth century under Llywelyn ap Gruffydd.

The name was spelled 'Haordine' in Domesday Book, which is believed to be a much mutilated derivation from the Welsh, meaning Castle on the Hill. It suffered as many changes in the spelling of its name as of owners, until it was acquired by Lord Chief Justice (then Sergeant) John Glynne, after the Civil War. It was his descendant, Catherine Glynne, who married William Ewart Gladstone in Hawarden church on the same day as her sister married Lord Lyttleton.

Gladstone, the 'Grand Old Man' who was four times Prime Minister, made Hawarden his home until his death 60 years later, and it is his name which is associated, above all others, with Hawarden. All through his lifetime crowds of tourists visited Hawarden to see the home of the great Liberal leader, and it is amusing to notice the enthusiasm, or scornful sarcasm, with which the hero-worship of Gladstone inspired nineteenth-century writers, according to their political convictions.

Hawarden is one of the few places in Flintshire where the park,

4 *Plowden Hall, Shropshire*

5 *Hanmer Village, Flintshire*

with the ruins of the twelfth-century castle, is open to the public. The 'castle' in which Gladstone lived was built in 1752, and like most mansions in the county, is opened only very occasionally in aid of local charities.

There are many Gladstone memorials in the handsome, but dark, church, reconstructed by Sir Gilbert Scott after a fire, and it gives the impression that almost too much money has been lavished upon it. Although Gladstone and his wife are buried together in Westminster Abbey, their white marble effigies lie on an enormous tomb, watched over by a life-size angel. Quite the most attractive thing in the church is the characteristic Burne-Jones window, with blue-winged heads of angels.

Near the church is St Deniol's Library, founded by Gladstone. The present building is part of the National Memorial to Gladstone. It is a quietly welcoming place, carrying on his conception of a library for Divine learning, with a house attached for the accommodation of readers, both lay and clerical, and of all denominations—or none.

Although completely overshadowed by Gladstone, two other people with widely differing claims to fame may be remembered—John Boydell, born here in 1752, who succeeded his uncle, the famous engraver and print publisher of the same name, and started a foreign trade which spread the fame of English painters and engravers abroad for the first time; and Emma Hart, afterwards Lady Hamilton, whose mother was a native of Hawarden, and who lived there, as a child, with her grandmother.

Two miles from Hawarden, along the Holywell Road, look for an inconspicuous sign to Ewloe Castle, which lies some 500 yards from the road, across a field, in a wooded dingle so deep that without the signpost it would be missed. A party of Cromwellian soldiers, lacking such aid, crossed a nearby field without even realizing it was there! Like all Border castles, it changed hands many times. The earliest surviving portion dates from 1200, when it was the southern outpost of Welsh rule against the lords of Hawarden. It fell into disuse after Edward I conquered North Wales and built his own great line of castles. Visitors coming from any direction other than from Flint Castle should be forewarned of a notice which says provokingly 'Guides to Ewloe Castle can be obtained at Flint Castle'. How-

6 Henry Wynn (d.1671), Sir John Wynn (d.1718) and his wife Jane, Ruabon Church

ever, even without a guide, the enchantment of Ewloe should not be missed, especially in spring or autumn, when the trees are at their best, and the many brooks murmur unseen through the undergrowth.

Northop (Llaneurgain) is a pleasant village with a church founded in the sixth century and entirely rebuilt by the mother of Henry VII, Margaret, Countess of Richmond and Derby, and, in right of her third husband 'Queen of Mann', who will be met with again in Flintshire. The church is beautifully kept, but has never provided a guide book when I have visited it, and its most interesting feature might easily be missed. Pennant's 'fat knight' is hidden behind the organ. To my mind, it might as appropriately be called the 'flat' knight, for although twice as broad as the other effigies in the church, he looks as if he had been squashed flat. All four effigies in the church date from the fourteenth century, but have not been identified.

There are pleasant walks from Northop along Wat's Dyke, here seen at its best, and the park of Soughton Hall stretches south from the village. The attractive old house is the home of the Bankes family, who are descended from Sir John Bankes, who was Lord Chief Justice of Common Pleas in 1640, and his wife the gallant Lady Bankes who defended Corfe Castle against the Parliamentarians.

William Parry, the Roman Catholic M.P. for Queensborough, who was executed for plotting the death of Queen Elizabeth I, was the son of a Northop man; and the father of Mary Ann Evans (George Eliot) was also born there.

Northop is at the meeting of six roads, one of which continues direct to Halkyn (Helygain), passing on the right the site of Llys Edwin (Edwin's Court, or Palace), a mound with defensive earthworks, which is believed to mark the site of the chief seat of Edwin of Tegeingl, from whom many of the leading families of Flintshire are descended.

Another road (A.5119) drops down three miles to the coast at Flint (Fflint). Traces of a Roman settlement have been found near Flint, which was probably engaged in smelting lead from Halkyn Mountain. Mentioned in Domesday Book as Coleselt, it was given the name of Flint when the borough was founded, from Fluentum, a ford at low tide.

Edward I advanced from Chester in July 1277, and set up his head-quarters at Basingwerk Abbey, with his supplies coming by sea, and a small army of foresters to clear the dense forest along Deeside. The castle is of special interest to students of military architecture, for its plan resembles those of castles in Southern France, and has no true parallel elsewhere in Britain.

Many famous men have been associated with the castle, but for most visitors it is Richard II, above all others, who comes alive here, with Shakespeare's unforgettable description of the meeting between the defeated king and the victorious Henry Bolingbroke, soon to be crowned Henry IV.

Until the Civil War, when castle and town were left in ruins, their history was bound up together, the Constable of the castle being Mayor of the town. Adam de Kyngeslegh, appointed Constable in 1371, is said to have been an ancestor of Charles Kingsley, and of several Denbighshire families.

The castle is now almost cut off from the town by the main road and railway between Chester and Holyhead, and in recent years, almost hidden from the landward side by housing developments, but it still looks seaward over the estuary with its bird-haunted marshes.

The Holywell road skirts the eastern side of Halkyn Mountain, which reaches its highest point, 986 feet, at Moel y Gris. The pre-historic hill fort of Moel y Gaer, at the southern end of the ridge, is between the lines of Wat's and Offa's Dykes. One of several possible routes for the Roman road from Deva to Varae and Kanovium (Caerhun) may have been along the ridge.

Holywell (Treffynnon) owes its origin to the holy well of St Wini-fred (Gwenfrewi), the seventh-century Welsh saint. Legend tells how a spring gushed up after a rejected suitor cut off her head, which rolled to the feet of her uncle, St Beuno. He picked it up, washed it in the spring and re-united it with her body. She became abbess of a convent near Llanrwst, where she was buried after her natural death about 650. She was re-buried in 1138, in a shrine in Shrews-bury Abbey.

The well is one of the 'Seven Wonders of Wales', all but one of which are to be found on the Welsh Border:

Pistyll Rhaiadr and Wrixham steeple,
Snowdon's mountain, without its people;
Overton Yew trees, St Winifred's wells,
Llangollen Bridge and Gresford Bells.

Like all such shrines, the well has been somewhat commercialized, and attracts large crowds of pilgrims. A superbly illustrated guide pictures even the individual carved bosses of the beautiful Perpendicular chapel, built over the crystal-clear waters of the well by Margaret, Countess of Richmond and Derby.

The parish church has a fifteenth-century tower, but the main part was rebuilt about 1750. Preserved in a glass case is the '*gloch bach*' (little bell), which was used to call people to worship. The church being on a hillside, the bells were inaudible in some parts of the town, and up to 1857, a bellringer popularly known as 'The Walking Steeple' was employed to walk round with the 'gloch bach'.

That stormy petrel, Frederick Rolfe, the self-styled Baron Corvo, spent the years 1895 to 1898 in Holywell, under the name of Father Austin, first painting a series of banners for the Roman Catholic church, and later, as chief contributor to the *Holywell Record*. It is impossible not to marvel at the complaisance of those who employed him, for his vitriolic articles set the town by the ears, and caused the newspaper's circulation to wane until it ceased publication.

Little is known of the history of Holywell castle, of which only fragments remain, and it is more rewarding to wander through the Strand Walks, where a part of Wat's Dyke is clearly visible, to the ruins of Basingwerk Abbey. The name is derived from the Weoc or fort of Bassa's people, which shows the site to be of considerable antiquity. Cenwulf, successor to Offa of Mercia, died there in 821, but nothing more is known of Basingwerk before the foundation of the abbey in 1138 for monks of the French Order of Savigny. It was the only foreign monastery established in North Wales under Henry I, and less than 20 years after its foundation it was affiliated to the Cistercian house of Buildwas in Shropshire. Giraldus Cambrensis records in his *Itinerary Through Wales* that he and Archbishop Baldwin spent a night there in 1188, but the ruins are chiefly of a later date, with some fine Early English arcading.

After the campaign of Edward I, Basingwerk lapsed into obscurity, except for a brief moment of lavish hospitality from the Abbot, Thomas ap Dafydd Pennant, immortalized by his guest, the Welsh poet, Gutyn Owain. This abbot subsequently quitted the abbey and married. One of his sons, Nicholas, was the last abbot of Basingwerk before the Dissolution. The ruins are carefully preserved by the Department of the Environment, but are now almost lost in the industrial development of Greenfield.

On a hill west of Holywell is the Franciscan monastery of Pantasaph, opened in 1852, where Francis Thompson lived from 1893 to 1897, with only short intervals, and wrote there nearly all the *New Poems* published in 1897.

Gorsedd, two and a half miles west of Holywell, is by-passed by the main road, but those who do not make the detour miss the delightful view from the summit of Rose Hill, which in good visibility ranges over the estuaries of the Dee and Mersey, Liverpool Bay, and the Cumberland Hills. I am told that with exceptional visibility, it is even possible to see the Isle of Man, and the coasts of Galloway and Ireland, but I have never been so fortunate.

Even along the main road, there are constant glimpses of the estuary of the Dee and the Wirral Peninsula. When storm clouds gather, and the tide is in, the estuary can look grey and forbidding, but even then, the white sands and dunes of the Wirral are luminous through the gloom, and on sunny days, with the sea sparkling, and the dunes gleaming white in the distance, it is a constant joy. When the tide is out, and there is only a winding, river-like channel, the greater expanse of sand is attractive, and to see the tide creeping in, is to realize how perfectly Kingsley described its almost imperceptibly rapid progress:

> *The creeping tide came up along the sand,*
> *And o'er and o'er the sand,*
> *And round and round the sand,*
> *As far as eye could see ...*

A pleasant road from Gorsedd heads north for Whitford (*Chwitffordd*). The church was almost entirely rebuilt in 1846, but still has

43

some interesting features, including a memorial by Flaxman the Younger to Thomas Pennant, a direct descendant of Abbot Thomas Dafydd ap Pennant of Basingwerk, and the best-known Welsh naturalist and writer of English prose in the eighteenth century. He travelled all over the British Isles and much of Europe, and corresponded with many distinguished men of his day, including Voltaire, Linnaeus, and Gilbert White. Twenty four of the letters in *The Natural History of Selborne* were addressed to Pennant.

Pennant's *Tours in Wales* appeared at exactly the right moment, when the beauty of mountain scenery (previously regarded with horror) was beginning to be appreciated, and was soon followed by a host of 'Tours' by English writers anxious to 'cash in' on the new craze. Downing, the sixteenth-century house in which Pennant was born, lived and died, was so badly damaged by fire in 1920 that it could not be restored.

Canon Ellis Davies, a former Rector of Whitford, wrote a detailed description of Whitford Church which has been reprinted from the *Transactions of the Flintshire Historical Society*, as a guide to the church.

West of Whitford is Garreg Hill, on the summit of which is Garreg Tower, half-hidden in woods. Long believed to be a Roman pharos, it is now thought to date from the time of Elizabeth 1. The magnificently carved Maen Achwyfan (Stone of Lamentation), the tallest wheel-cross in Wales, which dates from the tenth century, stands by the turning from Whitford to Trelogan.

Emlyn Williams, born two and a half miles away at Glan-yr-Afon, tells in his autobiography of his early schooling in Trelogan village school, before he won a scholarship to Ysgol Sir Treffynnon County School. A later pupil was David Lloyd, a native of Trelogan. One is still adding to his laurels with his Dickens 'Readings'; the other only lives now in the memories of those who heard his glorious voice, and whose highest praise for a tenor will always be: 'He reminds me a little of David Lloyd'. The little school has been enlarged with bright and airy classrooms to accommodate the children from a nearby housing estate—one of the all too few left of those superlatively good village schools of Wales which produced so many great men.

There is a road from Trelogan to the busy little harbour of Mostyn Quay. Mostyn village and Hall are hidden away in woods above the Dee. The Hall can be seen from a public path across the park. There has been a manor house on the site since the earliest times of the Welsh chieftains from whom the Mostyn family is descended, and Mostyns have played a prominent part in Welsh and English history. As kinsmen of the royal house of Tudor, they helped Jasper Tudor and his nephew, Henry, Earl of Richmond (afterwards Henry VII) to evade capture, and in all subsequent alterations and additions to the house, the window through which they escaped has been preserved, although it now only looks into another room.

The house was slightly damaged by bombing in 1941, but fortunately its treasures, including splendid paintings, Tudor and Stuart furniture, and the miniature silver harp awarded as a prize at the Caerwys Eisteddfod in 1568, escaped untouched. The valuable Mostyn manuscripts are now in the National Library of Wales.

A return to the hills can be made through the Devon-like Glan-yr-Afon, to Llanasa, a secluded village, partly in a shallow dell, and partly climbing a hillside. The church, although rebuilt in 1739, has some genuine earlier work, stained glass dating from 1500, and several murals with 'elegant inscriptions'. The neighbouring village of Gwaenysgor has a touchingly simple little church with a 'Devil's Door', and the oldest registers in the diocese of St Asaph, dating from 1538. The curious wooden arch in the south porch was rediscovered in 1951.

There is a delightful road from Llanasa to Trelawnyd—still marked on some maps as Newmarket, by which name it has been known since 1700. It reverted only recently to its older Welsh name.

The Gop, a quarter of a mile to the north, is one of the largest tumuli in Great Britain. It is clearly visible from the road.

Dyserth (Diserth), the older part of which is on the slopes of Moel Hiraddug, in the Clwydian range, has the unusual attraction of a waterfall in the centre of the village, which is rather too obviously out to exploit this asset. The water flows from St Asaph's well in the neighbouring parish of Cwm, and leaps 40 feet down the face of a limestone rock, to flow through the village street and skirt the churchyard. In 1774, Dr Johnson 'trudged unwillingly' to see it, and was 'not sorry to find it dry'. The mines which occasionally caused a cessation in the flow of water are no longer worked.

The many prehistoric relics found at Dyserth are now in the National Museum of Wales at Cardiff. The church, dedicated to St Gwyfan, a local saint, and to St Bridget, was entirely rebuilt in 1871. It is one of the few Flintshire churches I have found locked, but the number of these is bound to increase with the rise in vandalism in even the remotest areas on the Border. The church registers record the marriage on 27 November, 1624, of Bishop Parry's widow to Thomas Mostyn; of her son to his daughter; and her daughter to his son.

The ruins of Siambr Wen (White Chamber, or House), about 250 yards east of the castle site (one of several so named in the neighbourhood), are believed to date from the thirteenth century, and to be the oldest stone residence in Wales.

South of Dyserth is Cwm, 600 feet above sea level, and dominated by a massive church with a double belfry. There is a wishing well in the dingle nearby.

Dyserth is only two and a half miles from the sea, and a road skirting the seaward end of the Clwydian Hills runs to Prestatyn through Meliden, a village ruined by quarrying and much unplanned bungaloid development.

The spread of nineteenth-century hotels and houses, modern flatlets, vast caravan sites, and the usual paraphernalia of a modern holiday resort at Prestatyn, make it hard to realize that until the coming of the railway in 1848 it was only a cluster of fishermen's houses with an inn, now the Cross Foxes, where Mrs Piozzi (Dr Johnson's Mrs Thrale) came from her home, Brynbella, with other ladies of the Vale of Clwyd, to indulge in the new fashion of seabathing. Building excavations have from time to time revealed prehistoric relics, including the Neolithic skeleton of the 'Prestatyn Lady', a 'Pigmy workshop' dating from some period between the Old and New Stone Ages, groups of graves, and a Roman site with a bath-house and hypocausts. There are also sites of historic and Welsh literary interest in the district.

The caravans of Prestatyn are now merged into those of Rhyl, set at the mouth of the River Clwyd. It is one of the three largest resorts in Wales. The fine early seventeenth-century house, Tŷ'n Rhyl, is its only ancient building. It has been hidden by a maze of streets, and is threatened with demolition.

Sir Robert Jones was born at Rhyl in 1858. As a result of his experiences in military hospitals during the 1914-18 war, he enunciated the principles which led to the present emphasis on rehabilitation.

North of the road (A.5151) from Dyserth to Rhuddlan is Bodrhyddan Hall, in a fine park. The seventeenth-century house has a collection of armour, pictures and period furniture, and is open twice weekly from June to September.

Rhuddlan is strikingly set on a low hill above the River Clwyd, looking out over the low-lying Morfa Rhuddlan (Rhuddlan Marsh) scene of a battle in A.D. 795, when the Saxons inflicted a disastrous defeat on the Welsh. It is still remembered in the mournful Welsh lament *Morfa Rhuddlan*.

The ruins of Rhuddlan castle, with formidable round towers, lend distinction to the little town, which has only slight remains of its Priory, and of the hospital of the Knights Templars. The claim on the tablet on the old building in High Street that Edward 1 held the Parliament of 1283 and passed the Statute of Rhuddlan there, is disputed by historians.

A short walk along the river bank from the castle leads to Twt Hill (also known as Bonc Hill), which may have been the site of the earliest castles of Rhuddlan, in one of which Giraldus Cambrensis and Archbishop Baldwin were 'handsomely entertained' by Dafydd, the eldest son of Prince Owain Gwynedd, in 1188. Recent excavations have shown that up to 1277, Rhuddlan stood some distance from the site of the present town, and much information about Welsh villages before the Edwardian Conquest has been revealed.

A Sunday fair was held in Rhuddlan for centuries, but became the scene of so much immorality and drunkenness that the famous Welsh revivalist, John Elias, came there in the summer of 1802 to preach against it. He addressed the riotous crowd with such conviction on the text 'Six days thou shalt work, but on the seventh day thou shalt rest', that he overcame their hostility, and the fair was never held again. It was a typical instance of the immense influence wielded by the Welsh Nonconformist preachers of the eighteenth and nineteenth centuries.

Crossing the River Clwyd, the main road (A.525) runs south down the rich Vale of Clwyd, which still merits the enthusiastic description of Defoe, who was thankful to leave the mountainous region of Snowdonia for 'a most pleasant, fruitful, populous and delicious vale, full of villages and towns, the fields shining with corn just ready for the reapers, the meadows green and flowery and a fine river'. The A.525 continues south to Denbigh (Dinbych) but we turn left across the River Clwyd to St Asaph (Llanelwy), past the parish church, in the churchyard of which lies Richard Robert Jones (Dic of Aberdaron), a self-taught linguist who died in 1843, as he had lived, in direst poverty, although a master of Welsh, Greek and Hebrew.

The cathedral originated in a monastery founded about A.D. 550 by St Cyndeyrn, better known, perhaps, as St Kentigern of Cumberland, or St Mungo of Scotland, although his identity with St Mungo has been challenged recently by one scholar—and as stoutly upheld by others. Even his connection with the monastery has been disputed, but there is no question that his successor was his favourite pupil, St Asaph, whom he fondly called 'the Lord's little boy'.

Defoe thought St Asaph 'but a poor town and ill-built', but Dr Johnson, who must have been in an unusually gracious mood, admitted that 'The Cathedral, though not large, has something of dignity and grandeur'. He was right. Although the smallest of the ancient cathedrals of Great Britain, its fine proportions and its well-chosen site—it is the only ancient cathedral in Wales on a hill-top—give it a dignity worthy of its great traditions.

It would be a pleasure to linger over these traditions, but the cathedral provides an excellent guide-book, and it must suffice to mention the memorial outside the cathedral, to Bishop Morgan and his collaborators, who translated the Bible into Welsh, and inside, the simple mural to Mrs Felicia Hemans, the popular poetess of the late Victorian era, who spent many years in the neighbourhood.

Before leaving St Asaph, a thought might be spared for Sir Henry Morton Stanley (born John Rowland, at Denbigh), who was educated in St Asaph workhouse. According to one of his biographers, Ian

Anstruther, it was a 'period of terror and bondage', but although conditions were much as one might expect in a Victorian workhouse, his unhappiness may have been due largely to his own touchy and unfriendly disposition. Several local people tried to help him, and he certainly had an excellent education, which fitted him to become a world-famous journalist, although destined to be remembered chiefly for one banal remark when he met David Livingstone.

CHAPTER THREE

St Asaph to Wrexham

Leaving St Asaph by the road (A.541) which runs south between the River Clwyd and the River Wheeler, turn left to skirt the southern boundary of Llanerch Park, cross the River Wheeler, and follow a switchback road through a succession of small woods to Tremeirchion.

The Perpendicular church is the only medieval church in the British Isles dedicated in the name of Corpus Christi, but early records suggest this dates only from the sixteenth century. Mrs Piozzi; her father, John Salusbury of Bachygraig and his wife Hester Maria Cotton; and her second husband, Gabriel Piozzi, are all buried here. Dr Johnson, who stayed with the Thrales at Llewenny in 1774, visited 'Dymerchion' church and dismissed it with his favourite epithet as a 'mean fabric', but noted the texts on the walls were in Welsh. These have disappeared, but the detailed guide to the church records that by the mistake of a single letter in one of the Welsh inscriptions (cUrwch, instead of cErwch), the injunction of St Paul 'Husbands, love your wives' was converted into 'Husbands, beat your wives'.

In spite of Dr Johnson's slighting reference to the church, it has a great deal of interest. An effigy, traditionally that of Sir Robert Pounderling, Governor of Dyserth Castle, who died c. 1300, is said to be the earliest example of the wearing of leather gauntlets. Another effigy, in priestly robes, is believed to be that of Dafydd Ddu Athro o Hiraddug, an eminent fourteenth-century Welsh bard, grammarian, scientist and philosopher. His name is associated with the earliest surviving bardic grammar (llyfr cerddwriaeth), and with the Welsh translation of *Officium Beatae Mariae*, printed in the

Myrvyrian Archaiology. Examples of his poetry are included in the Welsh hymn book used in the church.

Among the murals is one to the Rev. John Roberts, who became curate of Tremeirchion in 1804, and vicar three years later. He introduced Harvest Festival services at Tremeirchion 28 years before the Rev. Stephen Hawker, to whom the credit is usually given, introduced them in Cornwall. More important, from a Welsh point of view, the Rev. John Roberts was an authority on Welsh orthography, and rendered notable service to the Welsh language.

There are three small panels of seventeenth-century stained glass with remarkable portraits of James I, Charles I, and Archbishop John Williams, which were replaced in the church after being found in the vicarage lavatory!

The fifteenth-century churchyard cross was taken down in 1748, and the beautiful finial sold in 1862 for £5, to pay for lamps for the church. It can be seen at St Beuno's College nearby. The cross was famous for its miracles, and was mentioned in an *awdl* (ode) written about 1500 by Gruffyd ab Ieuan ap Llywelyn Fychan of Llanerch. It is good to know the parishioners are not such vandals in the present day, and refused a substantial sum of money offered by an overseas visitor for the iron-studded oak door in the south porch.

The church registers date from 1590, and are full of fascinating details, some of which, fully annotated, are given in the church guide. Items showing the cost of living during the century 1700 to 1800 include ale at 6*d* a quart; keep of wife and child 9 days, 4*s* 6*d*; and two weeks' diet of a 'harper' at the Red Lion, 11*s*. A letter from London cost 10*d*. An undramatic entry of the birth of Jane Williams, daughter of a local farmer, in 1801, gives no hint that 37 years later, the child born in this remote parish was one of the party who witnessed the massacre of the Boers by Zulus at Dingaan's Kraal, of which she later gave a full account to Charles Orpen, the first Chairman of the Orange Free State.

The Tremeirchion caves, a quarter of a mile north of the church, were excavated in 1886. Both yielded the remains of prehistoric animals. Gerard Manley Hopkins, who studied the traditional Welsh poetic metres and greatly influenced English poetry by his experiments, lived for many years at the Roman Catholic St Beuno's College nearby. He pays tribute to the charm of its surroundings in his poem *The Valley of the Elwy*.

A road (B.5429) runs south from Tremeirchion to Bodfari, along the western foot of the Clwydian Hills to join the A.541, where the valley of the Wheeler cuts through the range. These impressive and shapely hills, recommended for conservation under the National Parks Scheme, stretch for 20 miles along the boundary between Flintshire and Denbighshire (Sir Ddinbych). A series of six fortified posts, dating from the Bronze and Iron Ages, along the range, has been partly explored and described in *Archaeologia Cambrensis*. The highest peak, Moel Fammau, rises to 1,817 feet, and is easily recognizable by the ruined Jubilee column on the summit, which commemorates the fiftieth year of George III's reign. Four parishes meet there, and the view embraces the estuaries of the Dee and Mersey, the Cheshire Plain, the Cumberland Hills, the Vale of Clwyd, Snowdonia and Anglesey. It has been suggested that the name of Moel Fammau (Mothers' Mountain) derives from Celtic mythology, which included a class of divine 'matres' worshipped by the early Celts.

The whole range is easily accessible, and there is the outstandingly fine ridge walk from Dyserth to Llanarmon-yn-Iâl, which is included in the Offa's Dyke Path.

Brynbella, the attractive house built by Mrs Thrale on her marriage to Piozzi, with stone from her demolished ancestral home of Bachegraig, is passed soon after leaving Tremeirchion. The gardens are open on advertised dates in June under the Gardens Scheme.

Bodfari is on the main road from Denbigh to Mold, and the parish is separated from Denbighshire on the south by the River Wheeler, and on the west by the River Clwyd, two famous trout and salmon streams, which have made Bodfari a haunt of anglers. It is delightfully placed at the foot of Foel Gaer, at the entrance to a gap in the Clwydian Hills, and surrounded by woods.

Only the massive thirteenth-century tower of the church survived the nineteenth-century rebuilding. Good seventeenth-century woodwork, including a magnificently carved pulpit, is preserved from the older church.

Beside the steps up to the church is the Dinorben Arms, much refurbished, but with the date 1640 over the doorway. About 300 yards from the church is Ffynnon Ddeier (St Defier's Well), in which children were put up to their necks, to prevent their crying at night. Another local custom in the seventeenth century was the offering of a cockerel for a boy, and a pullet for a girl, after nine visits to the well.

The B.5122 runs north from the Valley of the Wheeler to Caerwys, a breezy place in a beautiful region of small hills and woods, east of the main Clwydian range. The numerous prehistoric sites in the parish make it clear it was a populous region from the earliest times, although probably not the site of Roman Varae, with which it is sometimes identified.

The Welsh princes had a Court House in Caerwys, and Maes Maenan, about a mile south-west, was the site of a palace of Llywelyn, the last native Prince of Wales.

Caerwys was the only Welsh borough in Flintshire created by Edward I, and the pattern of the town then laid out is still to be seen in its long, wide streets. On the advice of Dr Thomas Wynne, a native of Caerwys, William Penn adopted a similar lay-out for his new town of Philadelphia, Pennsylvania.

The Great Sessions were held there until the middle of the seventeenth century, when the courts were removed to Flint.

It is said that an eisteddfod was held at Caerwys in 1100 under Gruffydd ap Cynan, Prince of Gwynedd, and there are written records of eisteddfodau held in 1523 and 1568. It is believed the judges at the first of these eisteddfodau received a commission from Henry VIII to call the eisteddfod 'to establish order and good governance for minstrels and their art ... and to grant a degree to such as deserve it'. The judges included leading local gentry and two celebrated Welsh bards, Gruffyd ab Ieuan ap Llywelyn Fychan, and Tudur Aled, nephew and disciple of Dafydd ab Edmwnd of Hanmer, who revised and confirmed rules laid down at the important Carmarthen eisteddfod of 1450.

The actual commission granted by Elizabeth I for the 1568 eisteddfod is still in existence, and also the little silver harp awarded to the best harpist.

This eisteddfod was re-enacted on the four hundredth anniversary in 1968. The proceedings were opened by H.R.H. Princess Margaret, and attracted large crowds. On the last day, the Gorsedd of bards, in their robes, with the people of Caerwys in Tudor costume, made a colourful procession through the main streets, and the Archdruid of Wales chaired the winning bard. It was the first time the Gorsedd officiated on such an occasion outside the Royal National Eisteddfod.

Caerwys church, which is chiefly of the late Decorated period, has some fine contemporary oak roofing, and a thirteenth-century effigy believed to commemorate a Welsh princess.

Angharad Llwyd, one of the most notable Welsh women of the nineteenth century, was born in the vicarage in 1780, when her father, the Rev. John Lloyd, the friend of Pennant, was rector. He taught her Welsh and Latin, and fostered her love of research. Her best-known work was *A History of the Island of Mona*. Her valuable manuscript notes on the history and antiquities of Wales are in the National Library of Wales. Unpublished correspondence reveals her to be no staid blue-stocking, as might be imagined, but a gay and witty woman. She removed to Tŷ'n Rhyl after the death of her parents, and died there at the age of 86.

Returning to the main road (A.541) along the Valley of the Wheeler, it is only two miles to Nannerch. The church was entirely rebuilt in 1853, but has some memorial tablets from the previous church.

It would be easy to pass through the large, sprawling village of Rhyd-y-mwyn without realizing its chief feature—The Leete, a four-mile riverside walk along the upper valley of the Alun, with its fine limestone cliffs and its woods.

An inconspicuous plaque near the entrance to The Leete records that Charles Kingsley frequently walked there, and that Mendelssohn composed *The Rivulet* in 1829 when staying with John Taylor, a mining engineer, who rented Coed-du nearby.

Mendelssohn's acquaintance with the Taylors had begun in London, but it was not until he stayed at Coed-du that his real friendship with them began. He came to Rhydymwyn on his way back from his tour of Scotland, where he had been overwhelmed by the scenery of the Highlands and Islands. He never saw Snowdonia, and explored only the immediate neighbourhood of Coed-du, and it must be admitted that the resulting *Fantasias* (Op. 16) cannot compare

7 and 8 Examples of wrought-iron work by the Davies brothers of *Bersham*. (Above) *The White Gates, Leeswood Hall, near Mold;* (below) *Entrance to Chirk Castle*

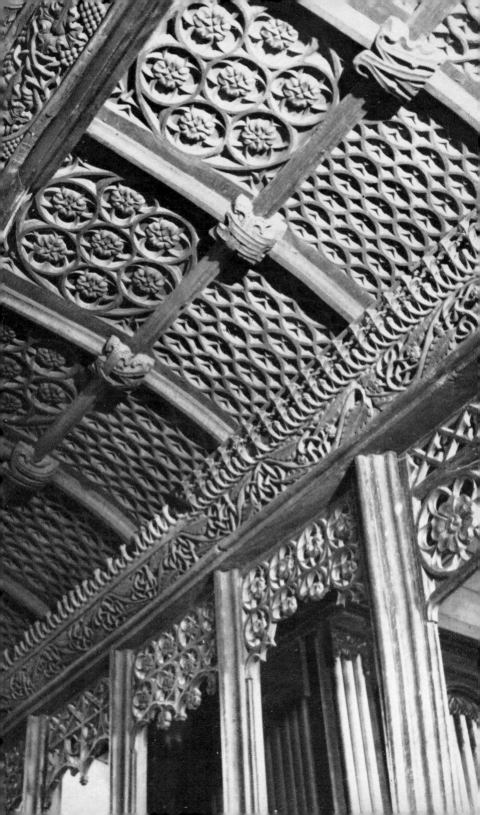

with the music inspired by Scotland. They reflect the quiet and intimate charm of life at Coed-du, into which the gay young man threw himself with zest. The origin of the *Fantasias* is described in a letter written by one of the three daughters of Mr Taylor, to whom they were dedicated:

> *The Rivulet*, which he wrote ... for my sister Susan ... was a recollection of a real actual river ...
>
> There was in my sister Honoria's garden a pretty creeping plant (*Ecremocarpus*) new at that time, covered with little trumpet-like flowers. He was struck with it, and played for her the music which (he said) fairies might play on those trumpets. When he wrote out the piece (called *Capriccio in E Minor*) he drew a little branch of that flower all up the margin of the paper.... The piece (*Andante and Allegro*) which Mr Mendelssohn wrote for me was suggested by the sight of a bunch of carnations and roses. The carnations that year were very fine with us. He liked them best of all the flowers, and would have one often in his button-hole. We found he intended the arpeggio passages in the composition as a reminder of the sweet scent of the flower rising up....

Mendelssohn himself confirmed this account of the origin and intention of these pieces. Although *The Rivulet* was long a favourite of his, only the second of the *Fantasias*, popularly known as *The Little Trumpeter*, is heard today. *The Rivulet* has been described as 'a typical melodious Mendelssohnian piece, very calm and cantabile, but with a feeling of movement and running water throughout'.

During his visit, Mendelssohn was greatly interested in the Welsh miners and their conditions of work, but was scathing about 'the harpers who sit in the hall of every reputed inn'. He also inveighed against 'all national airs', although he mentioned the 'beautiful singing'. He never revisited Wales, and never heard one of the really great Welsh harpists playing on the triple harp, which might have made him alter his opinion of Welsh national airs—but the visit to Coed-du remained one of his happiest memories, and he paid many visits to the Taylors in their London home on his subsequent visits to England.

9 *Fifteenth-century rood loft. Llanwnog Church, near Newton*

Coed-du is now a Denbighshire County Council Mental Home, but the walk along The Leete remains although much overgrown in places. Also, in these days, the Halkyn mines have been extended under the bed of the river, with the disconcerting result that, from time to time, the river runs dry without warning.

About half-way along The Leete there is a road to Cilcain, a little hillside village with a noteworthy old church. The elaborate fifteenth-century oak hammer-beam roof is one of the richest in the diocese. The principals terminate with figures of angels bearing shields, and the whole design is on a scale surprising in such a remote church, giving rise to a belief that it was brought here from Basingwerk Abbey at the Dissolution.

Loggerheads, at the upper end of The Leete, is just over the Denbighshire border, where the main road (A.494) between Mold and Ruthin (Rhuthun) cuts through the Clwydian range. The Loggerheads Inn has a sign painted by Richard Wilson, the eighteenth-century Welsh artist who was 'The Father of English landscape painting', and one of the founder members of the Royal Academy. He returned to North Wales after a career which brought him more fame than wealth, and died suddenly at the neighbouring Colomendy Hall, the home of a relative. It now belongs to the Liverpool Corporation.

The A.541 between Rhydymwyn and Mold skirts the southern end of Gwysaney Park, with its splendid mansion built in 1634. A more roundabout route through Pantymwyn skirts the grounds of Rhual. Opposite the south entrance, the Alleluia obelisk can be dimly descried across a field. It marks the traditional site of Maes Garmon (Field of St Garmon, or Germanus), scene of the 'Alleluia' victory, c. 447. The battle undoubtedly took place, although its site is disputed, and recent research tends to show that legends of St Garmon are a blending of the traditional records of two fifth-century saints: St Garmon, or Germanus, nephew of St Patrick and first Bishop of Mann; and St Germanus of Auxerre. The Britons, finding themselves greatly outnumbered by the pagan Picts and Scots, called on St Garmon to help them. He posted his newly-baptized converts on the hillside, and exhorted them to repeat his words. When the multitude of enemies approached, Garmon, bearing the standard in his hands, called three times 'Alleluia, Alleluia, Alleluia', which was taken up by a universal shout, which re-echoed from the surrounding hills, filling the enemy with such dread that they fled without striking a blow.

Mold (Yr Wyddgrug) grew up around the castle built on Bailey Hill by Robert de Montalt, a Norman knight who also held the castle of Hawarden. The origin of the name has been ascribed to the Old English for mound, or to a corruption of Montalt. It is now the administrative centre of the county.

At the time of writing (spring, 1971) it is still a typical Marcher town, with a spacious main street dropping down almost imperceptibly from Bailey Hill and the old parish church, but plans are in hand for a redevelopment scheme which will include the inevitable pedestrian shopping precinct and other adjuncts of 'progress'.

In spite of many fierce onslaughts, the first Norman castle proved impregnable until attacked by Owain Gwynedd in 1144. It was defended with great courage, but was eventually taken by storm and razed to the ground. It was rebuilt by the end of the twelfth century, but was again captured by Llwelyn the Great in 1199 when, as the bard Cynddelw gloatingly recorded, 'Alun ran red' with the blood of the enemies of the 'terror and torment of England'. It was a victory which recalled the triumph of Owain Gwynedd, and marked the beginning of Llwelyn's rise to power. After his death it changed hands several times before the Edwardian Conquest, and during the Civil War, it was occupied by Parliamentarian forces in 1643.

Bailey Hill is now a public park, with only slight traces of the castle, but the view from the summit is worth the climb. On a clear day, the greater part of the Clwydian range can be seen, stretching away to the north coast.

The parish church, dedicated to St Mary, is the finest in the diocese of St Asaph. There can be little doubt that Margaret Beaufort, Countess of Richmond and Derby, had a hand in the fifteenth-century rebuilding, for the Earls of Derby, Kings and Lords of Mann, held the barony of Mold from 1442 until the execution of James Stanley, Earl of Derby, in 1651. Arms held by angels on the corbels include a shield with the three legs of the Isle of Man, and they appear again on one of the columns, quaintly squashed in, with the bottom leg longer than the others. The Manx arms appear yet again in a window in the north aisle, together with the Eagle and Child of the Stanleys.

The tower of the church was rebuilt in 1773, and an apsidal chancel was added by Sir Gilbert Scott. The south porch was restored when the Disestablishment Bill was going through Parliament, and one of the pinnacles on the west side was recarved with a diminutive, but unmistakable likeness of Lloyd George.

There are good roofs, particularly in the nave arcades, friezes of small carved animals, and many interesting monuments and murals, which, together with those in the churchyard, will repay study by the collector of unusual epitaphs. Richard Wilson is buried in the churchyard, near the north door, and is commemorated by a window in the north aisle.

Mold is famous throughout the Welsh-speaking world as the birthplace and life-long home of the Welsh novelist, Daniel Owen. His mother belonged to the family of Twm o'r Nant, the best-known writer of Welsh interludes, and was a woman of remarkable personality, to whom Daniel Owen owed much.

His first two novels were read under the impression they were true, but his third novel broke down Welsh prejudice against fiction, and established the right of the novel to stand independently as a literary form. Two or three of his novels have been translated into English, but lose much in the process. His vivid characters and brilliant portrayal of the life of Wales during one of the most important periods in its history, have made his books even more widely read and quoted in the present day. He dealt with the turbulent days of the birth of trade unionism, when there was considerable unrest in the coal and lead mining area around Mold. In *Rhys Lewis* and *Y Dreflan* (The Small Town), he portrayed the division between the violent elements and the more thoughtful type of worker, and he did not spare the upper classes, who remembered the workers only at election time. *Gwen Tomos* has been acclaimed as his greatest novel; it was set against a rural background. He died in 1895, and is buried in the cemetery of Mold. His birthplace at Maes-y-Dref was demolished to make way for a housing estate, but is marked by a large stone inscribed with his name. His tailor's shop will be demolished in the redevelopment.

John Ambrose Lloyd, born at Mold in 1815, composed the hymn tune *Wyddgrug* when he was only 16 years of age. His cantata *The Prayer of Habakkuk* is said to have been the first such work produced in Wales. His hymn tunes, of which *Wynnstay* and *Whitford* are the best known, are still sung in Welsh chapels.

Another native of Mold was the Rev. John Blackwell, better known under his bardic name Alun, of whom the late Sir Idris Bell said he 'may justly be called a landmark in the history of free verse, although he also wrote in the strict metres'. Principal Thomas Parry, in *Hanes Llenyddiaeth Gymraeg hyd 1900* (translated into English by Sir Idris Bell under the title of *A History of Welsh Literature*), praises the simple elegance of his diction and style. His lyrical poetry was the forerunner of the Romantic Movement in Wales, and his poems are still recited in all parts of the Principality. He died in 1840, at the early age of 43.

Mold is on the banks of the River Alun, midway between the Dee estuary and the Clwydian Hills, in a fertile district from which the produce is brought into its weekly markets.

A mile down the road (A.549 running east to Chester is a tablet on the garden wall of a modern house on the left, commemorating the exploration of a cairn in 1831 (since demolished) which was the burial place of a Celtic chieftain, and the discovery of an elaborately embossed gold ornament. It dates from between 900-600 B.C., and is one of the outstanding relics of prehistoric gold-work in Great Britain, but there is some difference of opinion about its original use. It has been claimed it was a piece of human armour, but Professor Stuart Piggott and Dr Glyn Daniel consider it is more likely to have been a pony-peytrel. Whichever it was, it effectively disproves the old idea that the Celtic chieftains were uncultured barbarians wearing only the skins of animals. It is now in the British Museum, but there is an excellent facsimile in the National Museum of Wales, and Sir Hubert Herkomer used it as the basis of his design for the breastplate of the regalia of the Archdruid of Wales.

Three miles farther along the road to Chester is Buckley, which climbs a hill to over 500 feet above sea level. Welsh was the prevailing language there until the incursion of English labourers—mainly from Staffordshire, Lancashire and Cornwall—to work in the clay pits and coal mines. A unique form of dialect resulted from this mixture, used only by the people of the Buckley district for over 200 years. A history and glossary has been compiled by Mr Dennis Griffiths, a native of Buckley, in *Talk of My Town*. He has also written a book of personal reminiscences *Out of this Clay*, giving an intimate picture of life in this close-knit community in the early years of the twentieth century.

Buckley clay was used for making earthenware during the Roman occupation of Chester, and in more recent times, Buckley earthenware was even exported to Ireland, but now the manufacture of bricks, commenced by Jonathan Catherall in 1737, and made from the fire and acid resistant Buckley clay, is the major industry.

There is a most interesting group of stone manor-houses and mansions south of Mold. The oldest is Tower, built in the fifteenth century on to a peel tower which may date back to the twelfth century, and is complete with a dungeon and a suitable tale of savagery. Pennant tells the story of the high-handed action of its owner, Rheinallt, who hanged the Mayor of Chester from a staple in the Great Hall, during the Wars of the Roses.

Nercwys, hidden away among lanes a mile or two south-west of Tower, was built in 1638 by John Wynne, and is a charming house with a Long Gallery. It is now being restored to its original beauty. The village shelters under the Clwydian Hills, and the church has a Norman tower, the base of which has been fitted up as a Baptistry with panelled woodwork from the old pews. There is a sixteenth-century panelled pulpit, and an elaborately carved wooden chair, coloured in dark red and blue-green, picked out with gold, known as 'Cadair Fair' (Seat of Mary). It has been suggested that it is not of ecclesiastical origin, but was brought from abroad by Sir George Wynne, who died in 1736.

Most of the other houses of the district lie on or near the main road (A.541) from Mold to Wrexham. Pentre Hobyn was rebuilt in 1638—possibly by the same architect who designed the larger and more magnificent Gwysaney. There is elaborate woodcarving in the rooms, dated 1546, with contemporary furniture. A unique feature is the row of contemporary Lletyau (lodgings) built by Edward Lloyd for poor travellers after the suppression of the monasteries. By our standards, they provide very poor accommodation, but doubtless the Elizabethan paupers blessed him as a kindly and munificent gentleman.

Leeswood Hall (Coed-llai) was built between 1720 and 1730 by Sir George Wynne, a reckless spendthrift with an innate culture, typical of the eighteenth-century aristocrat. It was he who paid for the artistic education of his young kinsman Richard Wilson.

Jacobite relics preserved in the house include locks of the hair of the Old Pretender and of Bonnie Prince Charlie, tickets for Jacobite meetings, and portraits of the Stuarts.

The gardens of Leeswood were laid out by Stephen Switzer, a pupil of the designer of Hampton Court Gardens. There are magnificent rhododendrons of every variety and colour grouped around a tall four-sided columnar sundial, in the 'American Garden', and trees in the park include fern-leaved beech, giant Wellingtonias, and a very rare variety of tulip tree. The Mount is an eighteenth-century 'conceit' of three great stone seats (originally four), and a stone table, for picnics. The most famous feature of the park, the White Gates, 103 feet long, and of magnificent wrought ironwork, are on the road to the colliery village of Leeswood, and the smaller but scarcely less impressive Black Gates are beside the Wrexham road. They are the work of Robert and John Davies, sons of Hugh Davies of Croes Foel, Bersham, the famous ironworkers who were pupils of Tijou.

The Wrexham road continues through Pontblyddyn, and past Fferm, a stone Elizabethan mansion which was originally the seat of the Lloyds of Fferm. A milkmaid and a ploughman employed there figure in the ballad *Jennie Jones*, written by Charles James Mathews, and sung to the air *Cader Idris* composed by John Parry (Bardd Alaw). A decade later, Mathews included the ballad in *He Would be an Actor*, and it became so popular that Parry presented him with a silver cup with an inscription 'in the most elegant Welsh' to commemorate the event.

Mathews, who had been articled to Augustus Pugin, was lodging at Fferm from 1823 to 1825, before turning to the stage as a career. He was employed as an architect by the Iron and Coal Company at Coed Talon. Hartsheath Hall (Plas yn Hersedd), is of particular interest as the only one known to have been designed by Mathews. There is an amusing account of his stay in Wales in *The Life of Charles James Mathews* edited by Charles Dickens, son of the great novelist. Hartsheath, well hidden from the road by trees, has extremely attractive painted walls in the dining-room, and much fine Spanish leather furnishing.

Plas Teg, a little farther along the road, on the left, stands rather starkly in fields, only 200 yards from the road, against a background of steeply rising hills. It was built by Sir John Trevor, a scion of the Trevors of Trefalun, who was a protégé of Howard of Effingham, Lord High Admiral of England, in the reign of Elizabeth I. It did not follow the local style of the other manor houses in the district, but was a development of the great courtyard houses of the Tudor nobility, reflecting the ambitions of a court office-holder of the period. The Trevors seldom visited it, and the estate eventually went to a grandson, who also inherited Glynde in Sussex. He made Glynde (now famous for the Glyndebourne Opera House) his chief seat, and when the direct male line ended in 1742, Plas Teg was carried by a series of heiresses to the Trevor-Roper family. Each corner of the house has a projecting tower, crowned by a quaint wooden cupola with finial, giving it a curiously jaunty air.

Half-way between Plas Teg and Caergwrle, a road branching off to the right is the shortest of various routes to Hope village, east of the River Alun. It was once the centre of the Welsh cantref of Yr Hôb, and after the Norman Conquest, of the lordship of Hopedale, but changed hands more than once before the Edwardian Conquest, when it became one of the five Flintshire boroughs. Land was set aside for English settlers in Hopedale, which they rented at fourpence an acre. No Welshman was able to acquire any part of it without a licence from the Earl of Chester, and only then, if no Englishman wanted it.

In the course of time, there was some relaxation of the strict application of the law, but after the difficulties created by the Black Death, the English burgesses gained another charter from Richard II, which enforced their rights more strictly, and excluded even those Welshmen who had settled there, giving rise to great bitterness. This applied also to the boroughs of Flint, Rhuddlan and Overton (Caerwys alone being a Welsh borough) and it is interesting to find that by the time of the Act of Union, all the gentry of Flintshire, with one exception (Peter Mutton of Llanerch), were descendants not of the Norman barons or English lords, but of the old Welsh *uchelwyr* (gentry) and princes of Wales.

Caergwrle is an unpretentious place which derives its charm from its beautiful situation in a deep, narrow valley dominated by the precipitous wooded hill on which the castle ruins are set, with the steep Hope mountain sheltering the village on the west.

The ruins of the castle date from the late thirteenth century, and although its history is obscure, it is believed to have been built after the grant of the lordship of Hopedale by Edward I to his queen, Eleanor, from whence the village derives its other name of Queen's Hope.

The old theory that the castle occupies an early British or Roman site has been rejected, in favour of a suggestion that the site excavated at Y Ffrith in 1910, right on the Flintshire-Denbighshire boundary, is the Roman station referred to by earlier antiquaries. Offa's Dyke was built across part of the Roman site.

The Caergwrle bowl, now in the National Museum of Wales, at Cardiff, was found about 1820. It is a graceful bowl of black oak overlaid with gold leaf in finely tooled bands, about nine inches long by four inches broad, and two inches in depth. It probably dates from the sixth century B.C., and shows the influence of Scandinavian metalwork techniques on British metalwork of the Late Bronze Age.

A narrow, twisting road, climbing steeply through a new housing estate, leads from Caergwrle to Bryn Iorcyn, high on the slopes of Hope mountain. It was built originally in 1830 by Jenkin Yonge, and the fourteenth-century 'cook-house' was the nucleus of the existing seventeenth-century house. The Yonge family ended with two co-heiresses, the elder of whom, Penelope, was next of kin to Sir John Conwy of Brodrhyddan, and carried both estates to William Davies Shipley, Dean of St Asaph, on her marriage to him in 1777. Bryn Iorcyn became a farmhouse, and after a period of great neglect, is being meticulously restored by its present owners. The attractive little garden has a 'porthole' in the brick wall, giving a view of Caergwrle Castle and, on a clear day, as far as Beeston Castle in Cheshire.

Just beyond Caergwrle, the main road enters Denbighshire and reaches Wrexham.

CHAPTER FOUR

On the Way to Shrewsbury

*Maelor Saesneg, the Ellesmere Lakes, the Vale of Llangollen,
and the Hills and Valleys of Northern Montgomeryshire*

When Wrexham church was completed in 1520, the 'steeple' (actually a great Perpendicular tower), was hailed as one of the 'Seven Wonders of Wales'. The body of the church, which replaced an earlier building destroyed by fire, has a remarkable range of monuments, and much-quoted epitaphs. One of the most sensational monuments is by Roubiliac, depicting Mary Myddelton of Croesnewydd Hall, daughter of Sir Richard Myddelton of Chirk Castle, rising from her tomb at the sound of the last trumpet.

Elihu Yale, whose father was a Wrexham man, is buried in the churchyard; his epitaph sums up his career:

> *Born in America, in Europe bred,*
> *In Africa travell'd and in Asia wed,*
> *There long he liv'd and thriv'd; in London dead.*
> *Much good, some ill he did, so hope all's even*
> *And that his soul thro' mercy's gone to heaven.*
> *You that survive, and read this tale, take care,*
> *For this most certain exit to prepare,*
> *Where, blest in peace the actions of the just*
> *Smell sweet, and blossom in the silent dust.*

Elihu Yale gave books from his library, and a cargo of East India goods, to be sold in Boston towards the founding of the American college named after him. When Wrexham church was restored in 1901 graduates of Yale gave the roof of the northern entrance porch in commemoration of the bicentenary of the founding of their University. The entrance gates of the churchyard were made by the Davies Brothers.

Wrexham, the largest industrial town in North Wales, is close to the English boundary, and was originally in the Kingdom of Mercia. In spite of its Saxon origin, the town has been an outstanding centre of Welsh religious and cultural life. The Roman Catholic Bishop of Menevia, who exercises jurisdiction over all Wales, except Glamorganshire, has his seat in Wrexham, which saw Richard Gwyn, one of the Roman Catholic martyrs canonized in 1970, suffer for his faith in 1554. The town also has extremely strong Nonconformist traditions.

Walter Cradoc, when a curate there, inaugurated the rise of Nonconformity in the town in 1637; his disciple, Morgan Llwyd established Nonconformity in North Wales; and John ap John, the first Welsh apostle of the Society of Friends, was an elder of the Independent Church at Wrexham before he joined the Quakers, and evangelized all along the Border. It was he who arranged with William Penn that part of the Quaker Colony in Pennsylvania should be set aside for the hundreds of Welsh Quakers who left Wales to escape the bitter persecution in Charles II's reign.

It was this strong Nonconformist element which made the townsmen favour the Parliamentary cause in the Civil War.

In the following century, the Dissenters supported the Hanoverians, and the Jacobites in Wrexham, aided by miners from Rhosllannerchrugog, wrecked the two meeting houses in the town. Although most of the gentry were ardent Jacobites, they gave little or no practical help to the cause, contenting themselves with belonging to the North Wales Jacobite Society, the Cycle Club, which was founded in 1710, and was centred on Wrexham for the first ten years. Its headquarters were transferred from Wrexham to Wynnstay in 1720, and it survived until 1869, although purely as a dining and social club in its later years.

Roads radiate from Wrexham to all parts of North Wales and the Border country, and the smaller of the two detached portions of Flintshire is crossed by the shorter road from Wrexham to Chester. At first the way lies through the Denbighshire coalfields, to Gresford, a delightful little place, with a Perpendicular church so remarkable and so full of interest that it is a matter for wonder that only its bells figure as one of the 'Seven Wonders of Wales'. Outside, there is a fascinating frieze of small beasts, and inside much carved sixteenth-century woodwork, including the rood-screen, and unusually fine choir stalls with book desks and misericordes. The stone-work includes interesting effigies, and a sculptured font from Basingwerk Abbey, but the glory of the church is its stained glass windows, dating from *c.* 1500, which are the best in North Wales. They have been fully described by Dr Mostyn Lewis in *Stained Glass in North Wales up to 1850*.

Immediately beyond Gresford, the road and the pretty little River Alun cross the parish of Marford and Hoseley, a detached portion of Flintshire only 650 acres in extent. The black and white Marford Mill, painted by J. M. W. Turner, was rebuilt in 1791 after a fire, and is still in working order, although now powered by electricity. Here the River Alun curves around the foot of the low Rofft Mount, falling in a pretty cascade, before re-entering Denbighshire, and passing west of Trevalyn Hall, built in 1576 by the father of Sir John Trevor of Plas Teg. The history of the family, which has played a considerable part in national affairs, is told in *The Trevors of Trevalyn* by Enid S. Jones.

Rossett is set where the River Alun turns east to join the Dee, and Rossett mill is on the Wrexham side of the village. It dates chiefly from 1661, but has not operated since 1959.

The Pulford Brook marks the boundary between Wales and England, and the road runs north to Chester, west of the great park in which Eaton Hall formerly stood. It was demolished in 1963.

The longer route between Wrexham and Chester crosses the River Dee at Holt, site of a Roman fort, and of the most important Roman pottery kiln in Britain. Here the Dee forms the boundary between Wales and England, and has the curious property that at Spring tides it can be seen from the bridge flowing backwards. Farndon, famous for its strawberries and its plums, is on a low red cliff on the Cheshire side of the river. The church has some interesting stained-glass portraits of four leading Cheshire royalist leaders, with soldiers, weapons and camp equipment depicting military costumes of the Civil War period. The Barnston Chapel has an epitaph commemorating Roger Barnston of Crewe Hall, which lies a mile or two to the south-west. He fought in the Crimea and was killed in the Indian Mutiny. He is also commemorated by the Barnston Monument, a mile along the Chester road.

There are two main routes between Wrexham and Shrewsbury, one through comparatively little-known, but quietly attractive country, and the other almost entirely along the busy Holyhead road.

If the eastern route is chosen, it is well worth while to make a detour from Marchweil, with its modern industrial estate, and cross the Dee at Bangor-on-Dee into Maelor Saesneg (English Maelor) instead of the more direct route through Overton-on-Dee.

Approaching by road from Wrexham, the change from the flat countryside around Marchweil to the little wooded hills and valleys of Maelor Saesneg is evident almost immediately after crossing the river bridge. The name 'Saesneg' is indicative of the history of Flintshire's unique division into three parts. When Edward I took over the lands of the Welsh princes and formed the first Welsh counties in 1284, he excluded the lands of the Marcher barons, but Henry VIII divided these lands, with the result that Mold was included in Flintshire, and Bromfield and Ial (Yale) in Denbighshire; Marford and Hoseley were transferred from Denbighshire in 1541, leaving Flintshire with the 'islands' in Denbighshire which have persisted to the present day.

Maelor Saesneg is about 11 miles from east to west and six miles from north to south, and is almost entirely agricultural.

Bangor-on-Dee—a less attractive name than the Welsh Bangor-Iscoed, which means the 'High Choir in the Wood' and recalls the splendours of its distant past, is reached by a medieval bridge neighboured by the parish church with its Decorated chancel. The famous monastery is said to have been founded in the second century A.D. According to the Venerable Bede, there were over 2,000 monks living there at the time of the fatal battle of Chester, and over 1,000 of them, who prayed for the success of the Welsh, were massacred by order of the pagan king, Ethelfrith of Northumbria, who considered that if they prayed for his overthrow, they were warring against him. It was the end of the monastery, and the river having since changed its course, the site now lies beneath the Dee.

The site of Overton castle, once a seat of the Princes of Powys, also lies beneath the Dee, but the church still has the yew trees in the churchyard which were among the 'Seven Wonders'. Hanmer, in the south-east of the district, is an attractive little village set in wooded hills. It derives its name from the lake, or mere, of over 70 acres, which is really a part of the Shropshire lake district.

Hanmer was the birthplace of the great fifteenth-century Welsh poet, Dafydd ab Edmund, and Owain Glyn Dŵr married Margaret Hanmer in the church, which has since been rebuilt. Lord Chief Justice Kenyon was born in 1732 at Gredington Hall, which is still a seat of the Kenyons. The village also has many associations with the Hanmers of Bettisfield, a little village at the extreme south-east of Maelor Saesneg.

Worthenbury, on the north-eastern border, has a handsome eighteenth-century parish church which retains all its old box pews, including one with a fireplace belonging to the Pulestons of Emral Hall, to whom it was granted in 1282. Emral Hall, one of the finest mansions in Flintshire, was demolished in 1935, but its elaborate plaster ceiling has been re-erected at Portmeirion, in Caernarvonshire.

Ellesmere can be reached from Maelor Saesneg by way of the A.495 or by returning to the A.528 at Overton. Ellesmere, the largest town of the Shropshire lake district, has a pleasant jumble of narrow streets and old houses. It draws ornithologists like a magnet all through the winter, for the seven main lakes—five of which are within a circuit of five miles—are haunted by many species of wild duck, grebes, gulls, cormorants and rarer birds. As many as 2,000 mallard have been counted standing on the ice of Ellesmere lake. Naturalists are also drawn there by a curious annual phenomenon known as The Beak, which it has in common with a few lakes in the north of England. It is caused by algae which disturb the water for two or three weeks, and create a greenish or yellowish scum, very different from its usual clarity. In addition to the yachting on the lake, there is a little inland 'harbour' much patronized by cruisers on the Shropshire Union Canal, which links up with hundreds of miles of waterways in England.

Ellesmere castle has long disappeared, and the church has been largely rebuilt, but retains one of the finest chancel roofs in Shropshire. In the churchyard lies a man who 'saw seven kings of England and two Protectors' and died at the age of 104 after serving 'Mr Stephen Hatchett, his son, his grandson, his great grandson and his great, great grandson'.

Two miles north-west of Ellesmere is Gladlas Hall, where General de Gaulle and his family lived from October 1940 to September 1941.

The Shrewsbury road runs south-west from Ellesmere, passing several of the meres, to Cockshutt, north of which traces of Lake dwellings were found in 1922. Many rewarding digressions can be made from the main road, which continues through Myddle, clustering in a hollow of a rocky hillside. The parish was made famous by its historian, Richard Gough, who wrote its story in 1701 by first giving a plan of the church with every pew marked and numbered, and then a genealogical history of each occupant. The suburbs of Shrewsbury are entered soon after passing Battlefield Church, which marks the site of the Battle of Shrewsbury in 1403.

The more usual route from Wrexham to Shrewsbury makes an unpromising start through five miles of the industrial district of Denbighshire to Ruabon. The village is still dominated by the mansion of Wynnstay in its immense park, although the Williams-Wynns, once the greatest landowners in North Wales, no longer live there. A section of Wat's Dyke runs through the park, which was known as Watstay until the eighteenth century. There are elaborate monuments to members of the family in Ruabon church, including one to the first Sir Watcyn, by Rysbrack, and effigies of the Eytons of Watstay.

Within half a mile of Ruabon, the A.539 turns off for the Vale of Llangollen. At Acrefair there is a striking view of the great railway viaduct and the Pontycysyllte aqueduct and at Trevor, of the distinctive, castled-crowned outline of Dinas Bran, dominating the little town of Llangollen. There is no place in Wales better known than Llangollen, especially since the International Eisteddfod of Folk Music and Dance was first held in 1947. Competitors are attracted annually from all over the world, and even from behind the Iron Curtain. It is almost theatrically picturesque when the colourful costumes of many races are seen against the background of hills and

mountains, and those who flock to Llangollen must be filled with
wonder at the achievement of such a comparatively small population, in organizing and giving hospitality to so many thousands of
happy people during the week.

The International Eisteddfod is too often confused with the Royal
National Eisteddfod of Wales, but they are completely different in
their aims. The International Eisteddfod seeks only to promote folk
music and dance of every country. The Royal National Eisteddfod of
Wales, which is held in a different centre every year, and alter-
nately in North and South Wales, seeks to encourage Welsh literature, drama, music, architecture, painting, and handcrafts. Welsh is
the only language used officially, but in spite of this devotion to a
minority language, it draws even greater crowds than the more
widely based International Eisteddfod. It is a 'home coming' for
Welsh people to meet old friends, and revel in their heritage of
poetry and song. Any profits are devoted to the promotion of Welsh
culture, and by precept and example, and by practical financial help,
the Eisteddfod Council has promoted the founding of the National
Library of Wales, the National Museum of Wales, the Folk Museum
at St Fagans, and many other projects of benefit to the arts in Wales.

The work of administration is shared between the Eisteddfod Council and the Gorsedd of Bards. The Archdruid, who is always chosen
from the ranks of those who have won the 'Chair' for an *awdl* in the
traditional metres, or the 'Crown' for a *pryddest* (poem) in the free
metres, leads the colourful ceremonies of the Gorsedd, which add so
greatly to the attraction of this eisteddfod.

Llangollen was 'discovered' by travellers during the coaching era,
and its list of distinguished visitors increased considerably after the
opening of Telford's road, and the coming of the Ladies of Llangollen to Plas Newydd, in 1780. Everyone who has written about
Llangollen since then has mentioned the 'Ladies', but seldom without some mistake in detail. The latest, and by far the best and most
accurate account of them is given by Elizabeth Mavor's *The Ladies
of Llangollen*. Their home is now a show-place, although considerably altered since their day. They and their devoted servant, Mary
Carryl, are buried in the churchyard of St Collen's church. St Collen's
was restored and enlarged in 1863, during the incumbency of the

11 *Stokesay Castle and Church, Shropshire*

Rev. William Edwards, father of the first Archbishop of Wales. It has a fifteenth-century hammerbeam roof, elaborately carved with birds, beasts and flowers, and angel brackets, believed to have been brought from Valle Crucis abbey.

George Borrow has much to say of Llangollen, which he made a centre for many long walks and encounters with Welsh country-folk, and it is still a superb centre for some spectacularly lovely scenery. The A.542 branches off beyond the town to turn north through the Eglwyseg Valley past the tranquil remains of Valle Crucis Abbey and Eliseg's Pillar, a ninth-century memorial to an early Prince of Powys, and up the Horshoe Pass to Ruthin and the Vale of Clwyd. On the south of the Dee, the A.5 skirts the foot of the Berwyns before turning north-west to Bangor and Holyhead (Caergybi), but these are far beyond the Border country, and we must cross the bridge and follow the A.5 to Chirk (Y Waun), a pleasant village on the Welsh bank of the River Ceiriog which now straggles over into Shropshire. The great Border castle, a mile and a half away, is wholly in Wales. Set on an outlier of the Berwyns, it was built in 1310, and has been inhabited continuously ever since, and by the Myddelton family since 1595. The exterior is a unique example of a Border castle unaltered since the time of Edward II, in spite of sieges in the Civil War. It is filled with treasures, but as it is frequently open to the public between Easter and the end of September, the traveller can see its splendours for himself. Personally, I can never see it now without recalling the amusing story told by Augustus John in *Chiaroscuro*, when he came down to breakfast and found his host Lord Howard de Walden (a keen antiquarian) sitting in a full suit of armour and reading the newspapers.

The magnificent wrought-iron gates are one of the finest examples of the genius of the Davies Brothers. East of Chirk is Brynkynallt, seat of Lord Trevor, where the great Duke of Wellington, whose mother was a Trevor, spent many boyhood holidays.

The A.5 continues south-east, direct to Shrewsbury, but Chirk is also the starting point for Glynceiriog, the first of the series of valleys which seam the eastern slopes of the Berwyns, most of which are more easily reached from Oswestry. At its lower end, the valley is crossed by another aqueduct and railway viaduct. Both aqueducts were built by Telford to carry the Shropshire Union Canal over the Ceiriog and the Dee, with the Chirk and Whitehouses tunnels between them. Both aqueducts can be seen from trains passing over the accompanying railway bridges—and a strange sight it is to see a barge borne aloft beside the railway line; but to get the full effect of Telford's great works, they are better seen from the roadway.

Glynceiriog winds for over 10 miles into the heart of the Berwyns, some of which rise to 2,500 feet. Llansanffraid Glynceiriog, once a quarrying village and the head of a narrow-gauge railway, has a village institute which is a national memorial to John Ceiriog Hughes (Ceiriog), who was born in the valley in 1832. He was a versatile and witty writer of lyric poetry who achieved immense popularity in his own day, and is still giving pleasure, particularly with those of his verses which he set to old Welsh airs. Like all Welsh poetry, it loses much of its charm when translated, and he is best known outside Wales for his least inspired work—'God Bless the Prince of Wales'. Also commemorated in the institute are Huw Morys, the royalist poet so admired by George Borrow, who was born in Pontymeibion, a mile and a half from the village, in 1622; the Rev. Robert Ellis (Cynddelw), a nineteenth-century poet not to be confused with the twelfth-century bard Cynddelw; and Thomas Jefferson (1743-1826), President of the United States, who was of Welsh descent.

Relics of the old narrow-gauge railway, closed in 1935, are preserved in the institute, and a mile of the track, from Coed-y-Glyn to Hendre Quarry, given to the National Trust in 1948, is now a public footpath.

There is an extremely rough track from Llanarmon Dyffryn Ceiriog, at the head of the valley, following the upper Ceiriog, now little more than a stream, over the Berwyns to Cynwyd in the Vale of Edeirnion. It is impossible for cars, and difficult for all but the most experienced walkers.

A turning off the Holyhead road at Gobowen, four miles south of Chirk, leads to Oswestry, once the headquarters of the old Cambrian Railway, and of a network of delightful branch lines, but now without any railway at all.

Oswestry is one of the oldest towns on the Welsh Border, set between the pastoral plain of Shropshire on the east, and the Berwyns on the west. The fact that it is the third largest town in Shropshire is a testimony to the stubborn endurance of its English settlers, for it was always a centre of warfare in its earlier years, and was burned down by King John, and then by Llywelyn the Great in 1233; by Owain Glyn Dŵr in 1400, and accidentally in 1542, 1544, and 1547—which might have been calculated to deter the stoutest hearts from rebuilding.

The earliest settlement was the Iron Age camp on the summit of a hill to the north, now known as Old Oswestry, on the line of the later Wat's Dyke. The present town is said to have derived its name from Oswald's Tree, a cross on which the Christian king of Northumbria, St Oswald, was hung when he was defeated by Penda, the pagan king of Mercia. It is a belief which has been held for centuries, and is reinforced by the tradition of the curative powers of St Oswald's well. No lover of tradition will take seriously the view put forward in our own day that the battle may have taken place in Lincolnshire—particularly as this has been contradicted by equally eminent scholars.

The Fitzalans were lords of Oswestry soon after the Conquest, and obtained Clun by marriage with Isabel de Say, but hardly a stone remains of the castle where Giraldus Cambrensis and Archbishop Baldwin were 'most sumptuously entertained after the English manner in 1188 by William Fitzalan, 'a noble and liberal young man'. The parish church, said to have been founded before the death of St Oswald, has been largely rebuilt, but has some interesting monuments, including one to a collateral ancestor of Elihu Yale. The church is neighboured by the original buildings of the Grammar School founded in 1407.

There is a fine black and white house dating from 1604, with the crest of the Lloyds of Trenewydd in the window tracing, and the Wynnstay Arms is a seventeenth-century coaching inn. The Fox inn, another of the ancient inns of the town, had a gable which extended the full width across the pavement, but was shortened in 1870, owing, it is said to a guest from the Wynnstay Hotel colliding with it, and spoiling his new top hat!

Croeswylan Stone (the Cross of Weeping), once the base of a cross, marks the site where country folk came during a plague and washed the money they received for their produce in water contained in a cavity of the stone.

Park Hall, a vast prisoner-of-war camp during the 1914-18 war, was destroyed by fire, but the hospital was taken over by the Shropshire Orthopaedic Hospital, the first and most famous institution of its kind in the world. It was the crowning achievement of the life work of Dame Agnes Hunt and of Sir Robert Jones.

Sir Henry Walford Davies, who succeeded Sir Edward Elgar as Master of the King's Musick, was born in Oswestry in 1869. He was a phenomenally popular broadcaster and an able organizer, who did much to promote a wider appreciation of music. As a composer he is best known for the *R.A.F. March*, and the hymn tune *O Little Town of Bethlehem*, but he is remembered on the Border for the splendid work he did for the Montgomeryshire Music Festival and the Three Choirs Festival. He died in 1941.

Another native of Oswestry was Wilfred Owen, one of those gifted young poets who were killed in the First World War. His *Strange Meeting* is one of the most memorable of the poems of its time.

The Berwyn foothills between the Ceiriog and Tanat valleys rise over 1,700 feet, and are no place for the motorist or the inexperienced walker, particularly in misty weather, but the roads threading the Tanat, Vyrnwy, Cain, Meifod, and tributary valleys present no obstacles, and have every charm of natural beauty, and historical and literary associations. There is a direct road (A.483) south from Oswestry giving access to each, and to the upper Severn Valley. The road continues through some of the finest scenery of Central Wales to Llandovery (Llanymddyfri or, locally, Llandyfri), in Carmarthenshire.

The Afon Tanat rises in the Berwyns north of Lake Vyrnwy. Llangynog, at the confluence of the Tanat and the Eiarth, is dominated by Craig Rhiweirth, with one of the few examples of scree in the Berwyns. Once a quarrying and harp-making centre, it is still a purely Welsh village of stone-built houses at the confluence of the Tanat and Eiarth rivers. There is a wonderful walk over the mountains from Llangynog to Llandderfyl and Bala Lake (Llyn Tegid), which is also one of the few roads in the Berwyns practicable for motors. It runs through wild and lonely country along the eastern boundary of the Snowdonia National Park. The highest point, Moel Sych (2,713 feet) is shared between Denbighshire and Montgomeryshire.

Two miles higher up the Tanat, in the beautiful, lonely Cwm Pennant, which is filled with wild roses in the summer, is Pennant Melangell. The ancient church contains a fine fifteenth-century rood-screen, with carvings illustrating the seventh-century legend of St Melangell, or Monacella, to whom the church is dedicated. They show the saint giving refuge to a hare chased by a pack of hounds. The Prince who was hunting the hare was so impressed that he gave her a grant of land to build an abbey there, of which she was the first head. Some carved fragments built into the south wall and lych-gate may have come from her shrine. Southey, who visited the village, described the legend in a letter to his daughter. Not unnaturally, St Melangell is regarded as the patron saint of hares, which were known in the district as St Melangell's lambs. It is said no hares have been hunted in the district since the church was built.

Lower down the valley from Llangynog, the Tanat is joined by the Rhaeadr river, which marks the border between Denbighshire and Montgomeryshire (Sir Feirionnydd). Llanrhaeadr-ym-Mochnant, set in some of the finest scenery of Montgomeryshire, is especially dear to Welsh hearts, for it was in the vicarage that the Rev. William Morgan, afterwards Bishop of St Asaph, began his translation of the Bible into Welsh.

Rhaeadr waterfall (Pistyll Rhaeadr) descends over 200 feet in a series of leaps, the first of which is a sheer drop of 100 feet falling into a frothing pool, from which the second cascade emerges spectacularly through a circular hole in the rock.

Llangedwyn is the last village in the Tanat Valley before crossing the border into England. A road runs north to join the B.4580 at Llansilin, where the royalist poet, Huw Morys, is buried in the churchyard, a visit to which is so fully described by George Borrow. Half-way between Llangedwen and Llansilin, beside the Cynlleth river, is a mound surrounded by a moat, which is all that remains of the splendid house of Owain Glyn Dŵr, described by his household bard, Iolo Goch.

The river Cain also rises on the Berwyns. Llanfyllin, at the head of the valley, is a most attractive little market town of mellow red brick houses in a hollow of low wooded hills. It has old inns and Georgian and Regency houses, and an early eighteenth-century church. The old Council House, dating from about 1800, has frescoes depicting French landscapes, by Captain Augerand, who was a prisoner there during the Napoleonic wars.

Llanfyllin was once so noted for its ales that it was said 'Old ale fills Llanfyllin with young widows', but it is no longer brewed.

Llanfyllin is the nearest town to Lake Vyrnwy, a reservoir constructed by the Liverpool Corporation between 1881 and 1888 to supply Liverpool with water. Its newness has had time to mellow and it is strikingly beautiful in its cradle of mountains.

Five and a half miles to the south of Llanfyllin is Llanfihangel-yng-Ngwynfa, where there is a memorial to Ann Griffiths, who was born at Dolwar Fach Farm nearby in 1776. She died at the age of 29, but in her too-short life she wrote nearly 80 hymns which are among the greatest in the Welsh language, breathing a passionate mysticism and radiant vision.

Farther down the Valley of the Cain a road branches off to join the A.495, which follows the Vyrnwy to the wide Vale of Meifod, and the valley of the Banwy above Llanfair Caereinion.

CHAPTER FIVE

The Upper Severn Valley

Shrewsbury is one of those all-too-rare English towns which are attractive from every approach, even by railway. It is built on two hills, with an outstandingly beautiful skyline of tall spires and towers, and ringed with tree-shaded public parks and gardens sloping down to the River Severn (Afon Hafren), which practically encircles the town.

In some ways, Shrewsbury retains the 'feeling' of the Middle Ages even more successfully than Chester. Its narrow, winding streets and 'shuts' (the local name for the passage ways) still follow the lines of the Norman town, and possibly, are even older. Their fascination is enhanced by the extraordinary street names, many of which still defy the etymologists. They include such strange names as Wylie Cop, Shoplatch, Mardol, Meole Brace, Crowmeole, Barge Gutter, Dogpole, The Dana, Slang, and Murivance.

These streets must have presented problems even in the earliest times, and in the endeavour to meet the sheer weight of modern traffic much irresponsible and irreparable damage has been done. At long last, the Corporation has awakened to its responsibilities, and has prepared an extremely interesting and comprehensive survey of what remains, with practical recommendations for conservation, in which it is emphasized that the charm of the grouping is as important as the preservation of the buildings themselves.

In Grope Lane the gabled top storeys almost meet each other across the roadway. The Abbot's House in Butcher Row, which dates from about 1430, has medieval shop fronts which still show the wide oak sills on which the shop-keepers displayed their wares. Half-timbered houses in Wylie Cop include one in which Henry Tudor, Earl of Richmond, spent a night on the way to Bosworth Field in 1485, and the victory which ended the Wars of the Roses. Just above is the Lion Hotel, which was the centre of the social life of Shrewsbury during the eighteenth and nineteenth centuries. Paganini played in the musicians' gallery of its beautiful ball-room, Jenny Lind sang there, and Dickens, Hablot Brown (Phiz), Disraeli and other notabilities stayed there. De Quincey gives an amusing account of his stay, when he was accommodated in the sumptuous ball-room because there was no other room available. The Lion was partly rebuilt by Robert Lawrence, one of the best-known of the eighteenth-century innkeepers of Shrewsbury. He was largely instrumental in getting Telford's Holyhead road routed through Shrewsbury, instead of Chester, and in establishing the first Mail Coach between London and Shrewsbury. The inimitable Sam Hayward drove the Shrewsbury *Wonder* with such consummate skill that it took only 13 hours and 45 minutes for the 158 miles from the Bull and Mouth in London to the Lion, via Coventry, keeping such accurate time that men along the route set their watches as it passed. He would swing his team into the yard of the Lion without slackening pace, with only a foot to spare on each side of the coach wheels.

Shrewsbury's museums are housed in the splendid half-timbered Rowley's House, which contains a fine range of exhibits from the Roman city of Uriconium (or Virconium), and many other items of local interest; and in Clive House, part Tudor and part Georgian. The house was rented by Lord Clive, the Shropshire-born 'Clive of India', when he became Mayor of Shrewsbury in 1762. There are beautiful examples of Shropshire porcelain from Caughley and Coalport, iron-work, well-arranged geological exhibits, and the Regimental Museum of the 1st The Queen's Dragoon Guards, equally enthralling to the military historian and the least military-minded, with some life-size figures, and toy-like models showing the changes in regimental uniforms. The hours of opening are very restricted, but it is well worth the effort to go there.

It might have been expected that the defensive possibilities of the site would have attracted the Romans, with memories of their own city spreading over seven hills, but they settled five miles away at Uriconium—the present-day Wroxeter—and it was probably after the withdrawal of the Roman legions that the Romano-Britons of

Uriconium built Pengwern, a settlement under the sway of the Princes of Powys, which flourished until Offa, King of Mercia, defeated them and founded Scrobsbyrig, the forerunner of modern Shrewsbury (still pronounced 'Shrowsbury').

At the Norman Conquest, the town became the principal seat of the great Roger, Earl of Shrewsbury, who founded both the castle and the abbey. It is significant of the part Shrewsbury has played in Border history that its two principal bridges are 'English' bridge and 'Welsh' bridge, and much of its history has been in tragic contrast with the happy, friendly bustle of the present day. On the very spot where Dafydd ap Gruffydd, brother of Llewelyn the Last, was executed with revolting barbarity in 1283, the Duke of Worcester was killed in 1403, and the body of gallant, misguided Harry Hotspur was exposed for three days between two millstones 'that all might see and believe in his death', there was, at the time of my earliest visits, a large hotel, now replaced by a bank.

Shrewsbury School was founded in 1551, and its original buildings were completed in 1630. It has had many famous scholars, including Sir Philip Sidney, Judge Jeffreys, William Wycherley, Charles Darwin (who was a native of Shrewsbury), and Samuel Butler, the philosophical writer, best remembered for *Erewhon*. His grandfather, Dr Samuel Butler, afterwards Bishop of Lichfield and Coventry, was headmaster of Shrewsbury for 38 years, and laid the foundations of Shrewsbury's reputation for classical scholarship. In its earlier years, the school had a reputation for staging pageants and plays, and when Sir Henry Sidney, father of Philip, visited the school 'certain scholars apparelyed all in green' with 'green wyllows upon their heades' made 'lamentable oraciouns' so movingly that they caused 'many bothe in the bardge upon the water, as also people upon land, to weepe, and my lord Hymselffe to chandge countenance'.

The school was transferred to its present attractive site in the suburb of Frankland in 1882, and can be reached by the Chain Bridge.

Within the embrace of the Severn, but outside the town walls, is The Quarry, Shrewsbury's famous public park, including the Dingle, which is especially noted for its display of flowers. The Quarry is the setting for Shrewsbury's annual Musical and Floral Fête in August.

The Abbey Church lies on the other side of the Severn and can be reached by the English Bridge. All that remains of the great Norman Abbey is the church, partly Norman and partly fourteenth century, and the stone pulpit, on the other side of the road, which once stood in the refectory, and from which one of the monks read a homily while the others were at their meal. A mile away along the Holyhead road is the column set up in 1816, in honour of Lord Hill. It is claimed to be the largest Greek Doric column in the world; the total height, including the 17 foot statue, is 133 feet 6 inches. Lieutenant-General Lord Hill, born in 1772 at Prees Hall in Shropshire, near the family estate of Hawkestone, fought in the Peninsular War and at Waterloo. He died in 1842 and was buried at Hadnall, four miles north-east of Shrewsbury.

All Shrewsbury's churches have features of special interest, but St Mary's is the most beautiful and interesting, with a wealth of stained glass, including an enormous Jesse window of English stained glass dating from *c.* 1350. Dr Charles Burney, father of the famous diarist, Mme d'Arblay, who was born in Shrewsbury, was assistant to his half-brother as organist at St Mary's church for several years.

Shrewsbury is still an important railway junction, with a marvellous Victorian Gothic station, and it has long been a convenient centre for meetings not only of Shropshire Societies, but of Welsh Societies, and on these occasions, and on market-days, Welsh is heard in the streets almost as much as the Shropshire 'burr'.

Until the 1960's it was the pleasant custom for those attending meetings there to send tins of the delicious Shrewsbury Cakes (a local variant of shortbread) to relatives and friends, but this had to stop when postal charges rose so astronomically that the postage exceeded the price of the tins of cakes—a sad loss to local tradesmen, which has led to the ending of this once flourishing business. Now even the name of Palin is forgotten, although a footnote in one of the *Ingoldsby Legends, Bloudie Jacke of Shrewsberrie*, hails him 'Oh, Pailin! (sic) Prince of cake-pounders! The mouth liquifies at thy very name'.

Palin's own recipe was a closely-guarded secret, but a seventeenth-century recipe given me by an old friend probably resembles it fairly closely. The ingredients are 1 lb. each of flour and sugar; three well-beaten eggs, carraway seed and nutmeg to taste, and three spoonfuls each of sack and rosewater. These should be mixed together, rolled out, cut into suitable shapes, pricked all over the top, and baked on plates in a moderate oven.

Another recipe of 1765 varies the ingredients: 2 lbs. flour, 1 lb. sugar; four eggs, four spoonfuls of cream, and two spoonfuls of rose water; and a more modern and economical recipe suggests 1 lb. each of butter and castor sugar; 1½ lbs. flour, ½ gill of cream, 1 lemon, and 1 egg. There is also a recipe suggesting the addition of sherry, but there can be little doubt that whichever recipe is used, rosewater is an essential ingredient of the true Shrewsbury Cakes.

The easiest way into Montgomeryshire from Shrewsbury is to take the A.458 to Welshpool, direct to the border at Middletown without attempting to follow the long and seemingly endless loops of the Severn. Middletown lies at the foot of the Breidden Hills, so steep they are a stiff climb, especially after prolonged wet weather, when the footpaths can be as slippery as ice—and not nearly so clean, as I have had good reason to know. Although the highest of the peaks of Ordovician volcanic rock, Moel y Golfa, is only 1,324 feet in height, they have all the effect of miniature mountains. Moel y Golfa and Breidden Hill are thickly afforested, and Middletown Hill is cultivated or pasture land to the encampment of Cefn y Castell on the summit.

This is one of the numerous places on the Border where it is claimed Caradog fought his last battle against the Romans. Breidden Hill is distinguished easily by Rodney's Column on the summit, set up by public subscription after Admiral Lord Rodney, victor of Cape St Vincent and Dominica, died in 1792. It is often queried why this English Admiral, who had no connection with Wales, should be commemorated in Montgomeryshire. The only solution offered so far is that his ships were built chiefly of Montgomeryshire oak, and the subscriptions were largely from Montgomeryshire landowners.

There is a G.P.O. Radio Station at the foot of the hills, with a giant mast on the top of Breidden which is an important link in radio telephony to America, but undeniably an eyesore.

Daniel Patterson, whose *Road Book* ran into 18 editions between

1771 and 1829, thought the Breiddens provided one of the finest sights in the world. The view from the hilltops ranges over the Arans, Cader Idris, Plynlimon (correctly, Plumlumon, but practically unrecognizable to most English visitors in this spelling), and the Shropshire Wrekin.

Old Parr's Cottage on Middletown Hill was kept as a museum of relics of the old man, but when I visited it in 1951, it was deserted, and it was burned down in 1959. The path to the cottage was so steep that it made it seem more credible that a man who was active enough to live there could reach his reputed age of 152 years. A brass in Great Woolaston church, just over the Shropshire border, records that Parr was born in 1483, lived through the reigns of ten English kings and queens, from Edward IV to Charles I, and was buried in Westminster Abbey in 1635. Many tales are told of his superabundant energy, even in old age. He is said to have married at the age of 80, and at the age of 105 years had to do penance in Alderbury church 'in consequence of an intrigue with Catherine Milton'. He was taken to London by the Earl of Arundel to meet the king, and had his portrait painted by Van Dyck, but the dissipations of the Court proved too much for him, combined with the change to the polluted air of seventeenth-century London. It seems all too probable he hastened his end by joining in the dissipations! He certainly enjoyed his life to the full.

The road continues south-west to Welshpool, with Long Mountain on the east, and the Severn on the west. Long Mountain, a smooth whaleback of Silurian sandstone, reaches 1,338 feet at Beacon Ring. Like almost every summit around Welshpool, it has a prehistoric camp on its highest peak.

Buttington, now only an unimportant village at the foot of Long Mountain, is set where the road crosses the Severn by a bridge to join the road from Oswestry. Before the building of the bridge it had an important ford, Rhyd y Groes, mentioned in the *Mabinogion* in *The Dream of Rhonabwy*. The ford was of great importance in ancient times, affording an all too easy route into Powys. The Romans built a roadway; the Saxons beat back invading Danes there in 894, and were themselves turned back at the end of the tenth century, by Gruffydd ap Llywelyn ap Seisyll. Buttington itself had the doubtful honour of the only air-raid on Wales during the 1914-18 war, when a Zeppelin dropped a few small bombs and turned for home. A section of Offa's Dyke can be seen south of Buttington.

It was to bar the way to invaders that the great castle was built at Welshpool (Trallwm), originally known simply as 'Pool'. It was here the Princes of Powys, alone among the princes of Wales, survived the fateful year 1284. Spurred on by hatred of their Welsh rivals, they had more often than not been allies of the English, and wielded their power as English barons rather than as Welsh princes, as a result of their consummate, if not particularly admirable skill as negotiators, for the castle is so close to the English border that it is astonishing to realize it was never seized by any Marcher lord, and remained the chief seat of the Princes of Powys to the end.

The earliest castle stood on a knoll in the park, a quarter of a mile from the present Castell Coch (Red Castle) so named from the red sandstone from which it is built. It dates from the early fourteenth century, having been built by John Cherleton or Charlton, a Shropshire gentleman who married Hawise, sister and heir of Gruffydd ab Owain, the last of the male descendants of Gwenwynwyn. When the male line of the Cherletons died out in 1421, their heiress carried it to the Greys, who sold it to the Herberts in 1587. They became successively Barons, Earls and Marquesses of Powis. The sister of the last earl of the family of Herbert married the second Lord Clive, son of the victor of Plassey, who was created Earl of Powis in 1804, and is the ancestor of the present Earl: a too bare record of owners of Powis, many of whom had interesting lives, but none more romantic than Lady Mary Herbert, daughter of the second marquis, who married Count Joseph Gage. He made, and later lost, a million in the Mississippi scheme, attempted to buy the crown of Poland, and went hunting for gold in Spain. They were both immortalized by Pope.

Powis was handed over to the Treasury in lieu of estate duty, and transferred to the National Trust in 1965, but the present Earl still lives there.

It is the only place in Montgomeryshire open to the public. Its treasures, including many mementos of Clive of India, and its beautiful terraced gardens, have been pictured and described in many guides and advertisements. What they do not mention is the beer cellar, with vast casks sitting in it like fat aldermen on stools, each with its name painted on it—'The Duke', said to hold 1,400 gallons; 'Inkerman', St John', and others scarcely less capacious and oddly named. Oddest of all is the cask with the name of St David, the patron saint of Wales, who is famous as Dewi Dyfrwr—David the Waterdrinker!

Although somewhat overshadowed by the splendours of the castle, Welshpool itself is by no means without interest. It has a considerable amount of Georgian architecture, and some oddities; including a house on the corner of High Street and Church Street which has an inscription recording it was originally built in 1692 by Gilbert and Ann Jones, whose ancestor Robert Jones, of the time of Edward vi, is reputed to have been the first Welsh 'Jones'. The house was later occupied by the grandfather and father of Robert Owen, the social reformer born in Newtown. Some of the buildings still carry eighteenth-century fire office signs.

The church was founded in 542, and rebuilt in 1275, but was so thoroughly restored that although there is a long list of distinguished people buried in the church, not one of their monuments survives. The little black and white cottage nearby is now of far greater interest—it is traditionally the birthplace of Grace Evans, the devoted personal maid of Lady Nithsdale, daughter of William Herbert, first Marquess of Powis. Grace Evans assisted her mistress to effect the escape of the Jacobite Lord Nithsdale from the Tower of London in 1716.

Welshpool's museum, once a dusty jumble of relics of the Roman station at Forden Gaer and of the abbey of Ystrad Marchell (*Strata Marcella*), has been re-arranged attractively and expanded in recent years.

The other outstanding attraction of the town is the narrow-gauge Welshpool and Llanfair Caereinion railway. Opened in 1903, it was closed to passengers in 1931, but has been reopened by a band of railway enthusiasts. At present the 2 ft. 6 in. gauge trains run only between Castle Caereinion and Llanfair Caereinion, but it will be extended to Welshpool in due course. Hundreds of passengers make the five-mile trip purely for the ride along the beautiful Banwy

Valley. Llanfair Caereinion is almost certainly on the site of a Roman fort, but today is a placid little town, with all the dignity of a Georgian town, although some of its buildings are of later date.

Three miles north of Welshpool is the site of Ystrad Marchell, founded by Owain Cyfeiliog for the Cistercians.

Also in the neighbourhood of Welshpool are the encampment of Gaer Fawr (Great Fort), on a wooded hill, which was probably the chief seat of the old line of the Princes of Powys which ended in A.D. 855 with the death of Cyngen ap Caddell; and Guilsfield. It has one of the finest churches in the county, with examples of every period of building from the Transitional, and a beautiful carved and panelled medieval wooden roof. There are some interesting old houses in the neighbourhood.

The A.483 to Welshpool runs between the Severn and the Shropshire Union Canal—long disused in this region, but being restored near Welshpool for boating—passing near the delightful village of Berriew, where six roads meet. Berriew is in an angle between the canal and the Afon Rhiew, and it is well worth making the slight detour to see it. Set in one of the most fertile areas of the old Kingdom of Powys, between the sheep walks on the hills and the rich pastures of the Severn valley, it was also on one of the great Drovers' Roads, and a centre where wool was stored and baled, ready for the English markets. It remained a centre of the cattle and wool trade until the nineteenth century, and its many beautiful old houses and attractive cottages, in gardens frothing with roses, bear witness to the wealth and taste of its inhabitants in the Jacobean and Georgian eras.

Newtown (Trefnewydd) has many huge, converted warehouses surviving from the days when it was a flourishing centre of the Welsh flannel industry, and has a bustling modernity proper to the town where Robert Owen was born in 1771. No-one can dispute his claims as a social reformer who paved the way to a more modern approach to the relationship between employer and employed, although in spite of his advanced ideas, he was a despot—if a paternal one—in carrying them out.

The lasting results of his writings, and his experiments at Lanark, in Scotland, and New Harmony, U.S.A., are still not fully apprecia-

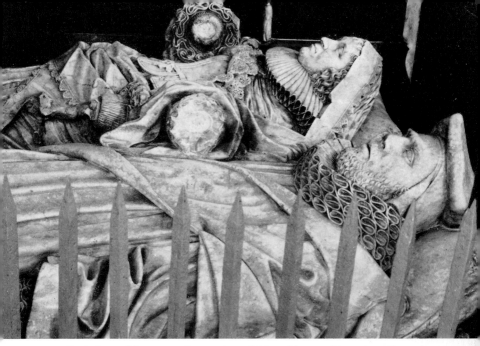

12 *Sir John Bridgeman (d. 1637) and his wife, attributed to Francisco Fanelli, Ludlow Church*

13 and 14 (below) *Sir John Kyrle (d. 1650) and his wife Sibyl, Much Marcle Church*

ted by the world at large, but the Labour Party has always been conscious of his pioneering work. In acknowledgement of the part he played in the foundation of their movement, British Co-operators in 1902 erected an iron railing, with bronze plaques depicting his social interests, around his grave in the quiet churchyard of the old church beside the Severn, of which only the restored thirteenth-century tower and roofless walls remain. Between the two World Wars, the Welsh nation gave a bust of Robert Owen to the International Labour Office at Geneva. Ironically enough, for a man so opposed to the spread of capitalism, the house in which he was born was demolished to make way for a bank. An upper floor houses a museum of Robert Owen relics.

Another native of Newtown, Geraint Goodwin, who was born there in 1903, became a journalist and novelist, and is best known for his *Conversations with George Moore*. He also wrote a number of novels describing life on both sides of the Border with sympathy and understanding. He died in 1941. Miss Eiluned Lewis, born at Glan Hafren, near Newtown, has re-created the scenes of her childhood in the upper Severn Valley in *Dew on the Grass*, a classic of its kind.

Llanllwchaiarn, which is now included in the parish of Newtown, was the birthplace in 1793 of David Evans, one of the glass-painters who were responsible for bringing back the medieval technique of leaded pot metal. He was trained and worked in Shrewsbury, being especially noted as a colourist. Examples of his work can be seen in St Giles, Shrewsbury, and at Welshpool and other places on the Border. At Llansanffraid Glynceiriog there is a good example of a background showing a special type of seaweed which is typical of his style; and some heraldic work, in which he excelled, is in Meifod church. He also carried out some excellent restorations in Ludlow Church, Shrewsbury Abbey and Lincoln Cathedral. He died in Shrewsbury in 1861.

One of the best known Montgomeryshire legends tells of Cae'r Fendith (The Field of Blessing), on the road to Aberhafesb, which belonged to Henry Williams of Ysgafell, a friend of the great Nonconformist preachers, Vavasour Powell and Richard Baxter. He suffered great persecution, but on one occasion, when all his stock was seized, the wheatfield thrived so amazingly that there were as many as eight full ears upon each stalk, and he was able to make good all his losses. He was an ancestor of Jane Williams (Ysgafell), the Welsh historian, who will be met again at Talgarth.

Newtown was known as Llanfair yn Cedwain until the sixteenth century, and was originally planned by Llywelyn the Last as a town with a protecting fortress at Abermule. It was destroyed by Edward I before its completion, and in 1279 Edward granted a charter for the founding of a new town to command this vital strategic centre, where the River Mule meets the Severn. If present proposals are implemented, the seven-hundredth anniversary of its founding will see the expansion of Newtown into a vast new town incorporating Caersws higher up the Severn—designed to prevent the depopulation of Central Wales, but which will almost certainly result in a further Anglicization by an influx of people from the Midlands.

Gregynog Hall, in the quiet hills four miles north-west of Newtown, was the seat of the Blayney family from the early fifteenth century until 1795. In 1919, Gwendoline and Margaret Davies, sisters of the millionaire Welsh industrialist and philanthropist, the first Lord Davies of Llandinam, moved there and made it a memorable centre of the arts, welcoming many distinguished guests, and even more students from all over the world with their own special brand of quiet, thoughtful hospitality.

The Spiritual Pilgrims, by Professor Ian Parrott, which takes its title from music composed by Gustav Holst for the Gregynog Choir, gives an insight into the all-embracing scope of their activities, but no single book could do full justice to all the creative talent which found an outlet there.

Sir Walford Davies, who was musical adviser to the sisters; Sir Adrian Boult, who conducted the Gregynog Festivals of Music and Poetry between 1933 and 1938; Ralph Vaughan Williams, Sir Henry Wood, Sir John Barbirolli, and many other distinguished English and Welsh musicians were associated with the Gregynog Festivals, and those at Newtown.

The Gregynog Press, founded in 1921, employed a brilliant team of artists, designers and craftsmen. It owed its existence largely to the inspiration of Dr Thomas Jones, a personal friend of the Misses

Davies, and produced about 40 or so books of superlative quality, before it closed during the 1939-45 war, owing to the paper shortage. These books are now eagerly sought by collectors.

On the death of Gwendoline Davies in 1951, the whole of the magnificent art collection which had adorned the walls of Gregynog was given to the National Museum of Wales at Cardiff. It embraced paintings ranging from El Greco to Botticelli, and from Richard Wilson to drawings by Augustus John, and was rich in the works of the French Impressionists.

Conferences were held for every cause which could promote knowledge or relieve suffering, and this work is still being carried on by the University of Wales, to which Gregynog Hall now belongs. The first Warden, Mrs Dora Herbert Jones, the Welsh Folk Singer, had been Choral Secretary and Librarian during the reign of the Misses Davies, and the new régime has been built on the lines laid down by the sisters.

Montgomery (Trefaldwyn), one of the most enchanting places on the Border, is close to the English boundary, and can be reached with equal ease from Welshpool or Newtown, but is utterly apart from either, and is to all appearances a purely English Georgian town of mellow red brick and half-timbering in this most Welsh of all the Border counties.

Although still nominally the county town, it is a placid little place with less than 1,000 inhabitants.

The size and magnificence of its fourteenth-century parish church is more in keeping with the town's ancient importance than with its present seclusion. The rood-screen was brought from the demolished abbey of Chirbury, and it has elaborate Herbert monuments.

In the churchyard is the grave of John Newton Davies, who was hanged for murder in 1821. He protested his innocence to the last, and prophesied no grass would grow on his grave in proof of the injustice of his death. Some writers have testified that after a long period, grass did eventually grow there. Others have found a strange, bare patch in the form of a rough cross. This I have seen for myself—but perhaps every now and then some lover of tradition restores the bare patch?

The town is dominated by the slight remains of the castle on its precipitous wooded slopes. It was founded by Roger de Montgomery, the first Norman Earl of Shrewsbury, but takes its Welsh name from Baldwin de Bollers, a Shropshire knight, to whom it was given by Henry I, after the fall of the house of Montgomery. The Bollers died out in 1207, and it passed by marriage to the Fitzurses. It was a Bollers heiress who was the mother of one of the murderers of Thomas à Becket.

It was a royal castle from the time of Henry III, and was a great bone of contention during the wars against the two Llywelyns. Although the town was sacked six times—on the last occasion by Owain Glyn Dŵr—the castle was never captured by force of arms during the Welsh wars, and was surrendered tamely to the Parliamentarians in the Civil War.

The greatest attraction of the castle is its associations with the poets John Donne, Edward Herbert, first Lord Herbert of Cherbury, and his brother, George Herbert.

No lover of John Donne's poetry can see the castle without remembering his poem *The Primrose, being at Montgomery Castle, upon the hill, on which it is situate,* and it is believed his ninth elegy, *The Autumnall,* one of the most enchanting tributes to an older woman ever penned, was addressed to Lady Herbert, the gifted mother of the poets:

No *Spring,* nor *Summer* Beauty has such grace
As I have seen in one *Autumnal* face.

It is probable Edward Herbert was born at the home of his maternal grandmother, Lady Newport, at Eyton-on-Severn, but that George was born in the castle. Edward, who was created Lord Herbert of Cherbury in 1624, is best remembered now for his egotistical autobiography, but he was also as much one of the metaphysical poets of the seventeenth century as his brother, and used the same subtle combination of Welsh and English literary forms of which George Meredith, Gerard Manley Hopkins, and Dylan Thomas were more recent exponents.

The entirely charming village of Chirbury, from which Lord Herbert took his title (although not the spelling) is only three miles from Montgomery, and is now two miles inside the English boundary. It was once a part of the Kingdom of Powys, and has the dual nature of a community half Welsh and half English which is reflected in the poetry of the Herberts. The King's Orchard, west of the churchyard, is traditionally the site of the castle of Cyriobyrig built by AEthelflaed, Lady of the Mercians, in 917. There is now hardly any trace of it, or of the monastery founded in 1180. Offa's Dyke runs through the parish, and many traces of Prehistoric and Roman occupation are to be found in the neighbourhood.

CHAPTER SIX

The Shropshire Hills

The most direct road (A.49) from Shrewsbury to Ludlow leaves Shrewsbury by the English Bridge to Meole Brace, which is now practically a suburb of Shrewsbury. The rebuilt church has some of the finest stained glass windows ever designed by William Morris and Burne-Jones, and a brass on one of the pews recording that Mary Webb worshipped there from 1902 to 1912.

Mary Webb struggled in poverty, and totally unrecognized, until the Femina Vie Hereuse prize, awarded to *Precious Bane* in 1924-5, brought her work to the attention of a small literary circle. Even then, it was not until Stanley Baldwin, the Prime Minister, praised her work in April 1928, five months after her death, that she sprang into fame almost overnight. Her death had passed unnoticed, and the tremendous burst of popularity faded after a few years, revived a little in the early 1950's, when *Gone to Earth* was filmed, and has now almost sunk out of memory even in Shropshire. It is significant that the first edition of the sympathetic, although not unsparing biography *Goodbye to Morning*, by Dorothy P. H. Wrenn, published in 1964, is still in print.

It was in Shrewsbury Market, where she and her husband sold the produce of their hopelessly inefficient attempts at market gardening, that she found the originals of many of the minor characters which live so vividly in her pages, although it was at Pontesbury, and later at her best-loved home on Lyth Hill, that she wrote most of her books.

The crudity of her plots, and her obsession in most of her novels, with the seamier side of country life, give a very one-sided picture, and her books are unreadable for many. It is the background of the legends, the scenery, and above all the wild life of Shropshire, observed with the eyes of a poet, which makes her books worth reading. As a distinguished critic said of the film *Gone to Earth*: 'Shropshire is the star'.

Continuing along the Ludlow road, Baystonhill is set at a cross-roads, one of which gives access to the low wooded height of Lyth Hill. It has a glorious prospect south over nearly all the hills and valleys which figure in Mary Webb's books, and north to the spires of Shrewsbury. The places she describes have been identified by W. Byford Jones in *The Shropshire Haunts of Mary Webb*.

South-east of Baystonhill are a number of small lakes, including Bomere Pool, the original of 'Sarn' in *Precious Bane*.

Soon after Baystonhill a road turns off on the east to Condover, which has several interesting old houses, and a church of creamy pink sandstone with the finest seventeenth-century nave in Shropshire. The unusual half-timbered gable of the south transept is particularly attractive. There is a remarkable range of monuments to the Owens, and the Cholmondeleys who followed them at Condover Hall, the grandest Elizabethan mansion in Shropshire. It was built by Thomas Owen, Justice of the Common Pleas, who died in 1598, before it was finished, and it is an outstanding example of the stone-mason's craft in the late sixteenth century. It is now the Royal National Institution for the Blind, and is open daily in August.

Mary Cholmondeley, the novelist, who was born at Hodnet, Shropshire, where her father was rector, described Condover Hall under the name of 'Stoke' in *Sir Charles Danvers*. Her best-known book, *Red Pottage*, was published in 1899.

Richard Tarlton, the comedian, actor and wit, who was a great favourite of Elizabeth I, is believed to have been born at Condover. He is said to be the original of Shakespeare's 'Yorick' and also of 'Pleasant Willy' in Spenser's *Teares of the Muse*.

The main road is rejoined at Dorrington, north-west of which is the unique church of Stapleton, which consisted of two storeys, built between 1190 and 1210. During the rebuilding in 1786, the two parts were thrown into one. A west tower was added about 1840, and ill-judged alterations were made during the restoration in 1867.

A mile and a half along the main road is a turning to Longnor, with a Hall dating from 1670. It is now a Country Club. The small

Early English church in the park has a remarkable open-air stairway on one of the massive buttresses, leading to the gallery. The woodwork includes a pulpit, a reader's desk, and box pews. One of the pews on the north side has the initials of Richard Lee, the village carpenter who made them, and the date 1723. His grandson, Samuel Lee, who was born at Longnor in 1783, had such an aptitude for languages, which he taught himself, that by the age of 25 he had acquired the elements of Chaldee, Syriac, Samaritan, Persian and Hindustani, and he eventually mastered 18 languages. He took Holy Orders, and was appointed Professor of Arabic at Cambridge at the age of 36; he later became Regius Professor of Hebrew. He also undertook work for the Church Missionary Society, and made scholarly translations of the Bible and religious works. At his death in 1852 he was famous all over Europe as one of the greatest linguists of his age. There is a portrait of him by Richard Evans in the Public Library in Shrewsbury.

The main road continues to Church Stretton through Leebotwood, where some of the Corbetts of Longnor Hall are buried. The village lies in the valley with its Georgian church a little off the main road, high on a plateau overlooking the surrounding countryside. It has a wealth of woodwork, including Jacobean box pews in the best tradition of Shropshire craftsmanship. Two curious features are a cupboard in the altar, and dragons on the roof beams. There are several half-timbered houses in the village, and the thatched Pound Inn has the date 1650 on one of its beams outside, and good panelling inside.

All Stretton is the first of the Strettons which derive their name from the Roman 'Street' which runs south along the Border from Deva to Isca and Caerwent. The Strettons lie in a valley running from north to south between the distinctive ranges of Caer Caradoc and Long Mynd (pronounced with the accent on 'Long', and 'Mynd' rhyming with 'pinned'). Both ranges rise so steeply they have all the effect of mountains, whilst their alignment leaves the fertile valley open to the sunshine.

The straggling, rugged chain of the Caradoc (Caradog) Hills embraces the Lawley, Little Caradoc, Caer Caradoc, Helmeth, Hazler and Ragleth Hills, consisting chiefly of Pre-Cambrian lavas, with small outcrops of rock, and rising to their greatest height in Caer

Caradoc (1,505 feet). It is crowned with a Celtic encampment, and on the All Stretton side has a small cave bearing the name of Caradog, but almost certainly without any historical association with that valiant prince. Caer Caradoc is best approached from its cwms on the east side, and rewards the climber with magnificent views.

These abrupt, angular heights make a striking contrast with the high, flat moorland summit of Long Mynd, which is covered with heather, gorse and whortleberries (locally known as wimberries), which colour it with glorious splashes of palest green, gold, purple and russet in their season. The Pre-Cambrian rocks of Long Mynd reach 1,696 feet at The Pole, from which on a clear day Snowdon, Cader Idris, The Wrekin and the Clee Hills can be seen.

The western slopes of Long Mynd, looking to the Stiperstones and Wales, is straight and steep and smooth, resembling the scarp of a chalk down, but the eastern side is broken by deep hollows threaded with rock-strewn rivers and waterfalls, known as 'batches' or 'hollows'. The Portway, an ancient track from end to end of the summit, is now metalled and possible for cars, but it is essentially a district which should be explored on foot.

Church Stretton is the best centre for the Carding Mill Valley, from which the Light Spout waterfall, and the wild, marshy tract of the Upper Light Spout Valley can be reached. Little Stretton is the nearest point to the lovely Ashes Valley, and All Stretton for the Batch Valley, which is thickly wooded with firs. Minton is the nearest point to the Callow Hollow and Minton Batch.

The Long Mynd is ringed with villages—Woolstaston on the north-east; Minton on the south-east; Myndtown on the south-west; Wentnor on the East Onny river which skirts the western foot; Asterton on the western slopes, with the gliding ground of the Midland Gliding Club on the summit above; and Ratlinghope (pronounced 'Ratchup') on the north-west.

Woolstaston has a diminutive village green and a church which was mentioned in 1272 as affording sanctuary for criminals. It has many interesting details, and much good woodwork of the 1860's, carved by William Hill, the local carpenter. This work was paid for by the proceeds of a booklet *A Night in the Snow*, describing the terrifyingly narrow escape from death of a former rector, the Rev.

Edmund Donald Carr—a warning to those who are too venturesome that the Long Mynd is not to be trifled with in bad weather. His little booklet has been re-published recently.

Woolstaston Hall, near the church, was the seat of the Pope family, but is now a farm. Above Woolstaston are tumuli known as Robin Hood's butts, but there is no known connection with Robin Hood, and it is more likely they were so named as a local tribute to Humphrey Kynaston of Myddle, who was outlawed for a murder at Church Stretton in 1491. He is said to have taken refuge in a cave in Nesscliffe, on the Holyhead road, about eight miles north-west of Shrewsbury. He earned a reputation for robbing the rich to give to the poor, and countless legends grew up around his name, which have been recounted by Charlotte Burne in *Shropshire Folklore*.

The hamlet of Minton seems to have let time go by, for to this day its arrangement is so akin to that of the original Saxon settlers that it needs little effort to picture them, with their cottages and small-holdings, clustering round the village green in the protection of the manor-house, and the neighbouring castle of which only the great mound survives. The very fact that there is no church at Minton is a reminder that the Saxons were pagans when they first settled in Britain.

Over the hill is Myndtown, on a knoll overlooking the valley of the East Onny river. It is a mere hamlet, with a church, farmhouse and rectory. The church is ancient, but of no particular architectural interest, and its chief attraction is the large Jacobean manorial pew, and the curious font, which is made up of four pieces with traces of a hinge and lock, and may date back to the twelfth century.

Myndtown blocks the end of a lane running directly west to cross the river Onny and join the road skirting the southern end of Long Mynd, and north to Wentnor, breezily set on one of the foothills. Its church was rebuilt in 1885, re-using much of the ancient material, but its chief interest is the 'Hurricane Gravestone' in the churchyard. It commemorates a tragedy in 1772, when a house in the neighbouring hamlet of Asterton was blown away and three of the people sleeping in it were killed instantly, and others buried under the rubble. The company had assembled for a 'caking', a common event in those times, when a cottager would brew a barrel of ale, and make a supply of cakes and anyone, by paying an entrance fee, might share in the night's carouse.

There is a road giving spectacularly beautiful views crossing the Long Mynd from Asterton to Church Stretton, possible, but hair-raising for motorists, and far better followed on foot, though this is admittedly strenuous in parts.

Ratlinghope, hidden in a deep fold of the hills, and reached by narrow winding lanes, is sometimes completely cut off from the world in winter. There is now no trace of the priory of Augustinian Canons, which was connected with the abbey of Wigmore in Herefordshire, and enjoyed the special protection of Llywelyn the Great. The simple and unpretentious little church has two curious connections with the outer world—one of the two fonts was brought from Alderbury, Salisbury, in 1890; and the heating apparatus was once used in Windsor Castle. There are prehistoric camps on the neighbouring hills, and the steep road to the summit of Long Mynd gives wonderful views of the rocky outcrop of the Stiperstones.

Most people explore Long Mynd from one of the Strettons strung out along the main road on the west of the range. They achieved a mild fame as spas in the Victorian era, and seem to have had a special attraction for minor Victorian novelists. Sarah Smith, who was born at Wellington, Shropshire, in 1832, took her pen-name of Hesba Stretton from the initials of her surviving brothers and sisters, combined with 'Stretton' from All Stretton, where her youngest sister had inherited property. Hesba Stretton visited All Stretton annually until her death, although she had removed to London in 1870. She was befriended by Dickens, who published some of her stories in *Household Words*, and she contributed to nearly every Christmas number of *All the Year Round*. She was associated with Baroness Burdett-Coutts in works of charity, and took a prominent part in founding the London Society for the Prevention of Cruelty to Children, later the S.P.C.C.

Her best-known book was *Jessica's First Prayer*. When remembered at all now, it is often derided, especially by those who have never read it, but it was a serious work from first-hand study of the life of destitute children in the slum conditions of large cities, and was commended by Lord Shaftesbury. Another of her novels, *Alone in London*, also achieved considerable success. She died in 1911, and her association with the district is commemorated with a diminutive window in the south transept of Church Stretton church, with a figure in green representing the heroine of *Jessica's First Prayer*.

Another earnest Victorian woman novelist, Beatrice Harraden (1864-1930), who worked for female emancipation, wrote with sentimental pathos in her most successful book, *Ships that Pass in the Night*. She used Little Stretton as the setting for a short story *The Green Dragon*.

The Rev. John Watson ('Ian Maclaren') frequently stayed at the half-timbered Tan House at Little Stretton whilst writing his novels, which although now contemptuously dismissed as 'kailyard', are true to Scottish character as far as they go.

Stretton, by that much under-rated novelist, Henry Kingsley, had a Shropshire background.

All Stretton, which is believed to take the first part of its name from a corruption of Alured, the original Saxon owner, has several good sixteenth-century black and white houses.

Church Stretton owes much to its background of hills, but is a delightful place of spacious streets and a prevailing air of peace, which is a testimony to the taste of its Victorian builders. Almost all its pretty, half-timbered houses are of Victorian origin, but the Early English church has a Norman nave, and there is a Sheil-na-grig (a fertility figure) above the north doorway. The woodwork is Jacobean, and there is some sixteenth- and seventeenth-century Flemish glass, and more modern windows commemorating not only Hesba Stretton, but Lord Leighton, whose ancestors came from Shropshire. He took his territorial title from Stretton. The first and last Lord Leighton, sculptor, painter, and President of the Royal Academy, died at the age of 65, the day after the title was conferred, and his peerage, which existed for a single day is unique.

The main road, the old Roman road, the Quinney Brook, and the railway, all run through the eastern end of Church Stretton, skirting Ragleth Hill to Little Stretton. Between the two is the site of Brockhurst Castle, which has provoked conflicting opinions as to whether it was originally Roman or Saxon. It was a royal fortress in Norman times, and was repaired in 1238, but dismantled less than

20 years later, and was in ruins when Camden saw it.

Little Stretton is set in the narrowest part of the valley, and has some notable timber-framed houses. The Manor House dates from 1600; the Malt House has a large, weather-boarded barn; and Tan House is attractive although rather over-restored. The church, built in 1903, blends with these houses, and is one of the few thatched churches. The most attractive part of the village is just off the main road, where secluded cottages shelter under the lower slopes of Long Mynd, and are reached by small bridges across a cascading stream. The Ragleth Inn saw the performances of the traditional open-air plays which were popular a century or more ago, when travelling actors set up their stage on a couple of wagons, and gave their performances which, although seldom of great merit, were extremely popular with the country folk who flocked to them.

The road from Little Stretton keeps company with the Quinney Brook south to its junction with the A.489 to Newtown, and the confluence of the Quinney with the River Onny. Nearby is Wistanstow, where Wystan, grandson of Wiflaf, King of Mercia, was murdered in 849. The story is told by Thomas de Marleberge, Abbot of Evesham, in *The Chronica Abbatae de Evesham*. Wystan was called upon to succeed his grandfather, but refused, 'wishing to become an heir of a heavenly kingdom'. He committed the care of the kingdom to his mother Elfleda, and the chief men of the land, but his uncle Bertulph was 'inflamed with a desire of ruling and with a sinful love for the queen-regent', and Wystan was stabbed whilst giving the kiss of peace. The body was conveyed to Repton in Derbyshire, and buried, but for '30 days a column of light extending from the spot where he was slain to the heavens above, was seen by all those who dwelt there, and every year, on the day of his martyrdom, the hairs of his head, severed by the sword, sprang up like grass'. Such convincing signs of sanctity could not be ignored, and a church was built, to which pilgrims resorted to see the annual growth of the hair. No trace of the Saxon building remains—nor has anyone seen the hair, which is not surprising, as the present church at Wistanstow is not even dedicated to Wystan, but to the Holy Trinity, with the usual Norman contempt for any saints but their own. However, St Wystan can be seen as a golden-haired boy in a red cloak, and his mother, in purple, white and gold, in one of the windows.

The Ludlow road continues south along the Valley of the Onny to Craven Arms, still, at the time of writing, the junction of the Central Wales Railway and the railway between Newport and Chester. Craven Arms is also at an important cross-roads, and the hotel was mentioned in the *Cambrian Travellers' Guide and Pocket Companion* of 1808 as 'an excellent inn lately built at the expense of the Lord Craven'. The obelisk in front of the hotel gives distances which show it was set up before the opening of Telford's Holyhead road in 1826.

Such a date would presuppose a place of some charm, but Craven Arms has never taken itself seriously as a holiday centre. It has little accommodation and straggles haphazardly, with a series of stock-yards, timber yards, and machinery depots, and it is better to continue down the Onny valley where, only a mile away, there is an enchanting contrast in Stokesay Castle—quite my favourite small castle of the British Isles. The past can be re-created there without conscious effort, for it escaped damage during the Civil War, when the royalist garrison surrendered tamely.

The strikingly picturesque group of church, hall and gatehouse ranges in date from Norman to Elizabethan. The Great Hall was almost entirely built between 1270 and 1280, and is remarkable for the great size of its windows. Only in England at that date would it have been possible to feel such security. Although it is the earliest fortified manor-house in the country, it was built too late to share in any of the historical events of the Welsh wars, and was one of the first attempts to outshine the neighbours now known as 'keeping up with the Joneses'. It soon pointed the way to greater comfort and convenience along the western line of fortresses on the Border. The Says of Clun were the first to hold Stokesay, and were succeeded by the Ludlows.

The elaborate half-timbered Elizabethan gatehouse is in strong contrast with the grey stone church and castle. Only the northern tower of the castle has half-timbering—a later and somewhat incongruous, but wholly endearing upper storey, strongly reminiscent of an illustration to Grimms' *Fairy Tales*.

There is some splendid woodwork in the church, including a pulpit with tester, and a canopied pew. Stokesay is open regularly to the public all the year round.

Continuing down the Onny Valley, Bromfield, where the Onny flows into the River Teme, had a collegiate church in Saxon times, which became monastic in 1135. It stood on the peninsula formed by the Teme and Onny, but very little remains, apart from the Gatehouse and the splendid church—a remarkable building, with traces of Norman work. It has some carving, said to have come from Ludlow castle; a painted plaster ceiling which has been called 'the best example of the worst style of ecclesiastical art', painted in 1672; and good modern carving. The property was granted to Charles Fox at the Dissolution, and he included the chancel in the house he built. The chancel was restored for Divine service in 1658, and traces of the mullioned windows of Fox's bed-room and dining-room can be seen on the east wall.

A stone in the churchyard bids the visitor 'honour a physician with the honour due to him'. It commemorates Henry Hickman, who was the first man to discover the use of anaesthetics, but died at the age of 30, without being able to persuade the medical faculty of the value of his discovery. He was a member of the Royal College of Surgeons before he was 21, and began to practice in Ludlow. He offered his discovery to the Royal Society, and then to the French Academy of Medicine, without wish for monetary reward, but neither accepted. Others had the credit when chloroform was first employed as an anaesthetic in 1847, and it was not until 1913, when Henry Wellcome formed his Historical Medical Museum in London, that Hickman's part as a discoverer was realized. The centenary of his death was celebrated in 1930.

It is only a short distance along the valley of the Teme from Bromfield to Ludlow.

Ludlow can also be reached from Shrewsbury by the A.488, a slightly longer but rather less frequented route through Pontesford (pronounced in three syllables) and Pontesbury (pronounced Pontsbury). *The Anglo-Saxon Chronicle* records a battle here in 661, between Cenwulf, King of the West Saxons, and Wulfere, King of Mercia, and possibly the camps on Pontesford and Pontesbury Hills are connected with this conflict.

The isolated Pontesford Hill, split into two peaks, rises steeply above the village. Its volcanic rocks are similar to those of Caer Caradoc, and there are magnificent views over Wales and Shropshire from the summit. The lower slopes have been thickly planted by the Forestry Commission, but the upper slopes are grass-covered, and the Pontesford peak can be distinguished by the thin, straggling line of trees extending along the top of the ridge like a mane.

About 100 acres of the Earl's Hill peak have been leased from the Chitty family as the first Nature Reserve in Shropshire set up by the Shropshire Conservation Trust. The hill is of great geological interest for the many varieties of rocks represented, and there are rare plants on the grassy slopes and sheer rock faces, which are also the haunt of many species of birds.

Until 1914, crowds of people used to climb Pontesford Hill on Palm Sunday, to look for the Golden Arrow, said to have been dropped by a king—or a fairy—or in battle (there are many versions), which would be recovered only by a destined heir to an estate, or by the seventh daughter of a seventh son, searching for it at midnight. In earlier times the search ended in a 'wake' or merry-making of unbridled licence. The local school children still carry on the tradition on Palm Sundays, but in more decorous fashion.

Directly south of Pontesbury is the village of Habberley. The Hall, a timber-framed house dated 1593, with tall chimney stacks and huge brick barns, was the home of William Mytton, an eighteenth-century Shropshire historian, who was one of the family of Shropshire squires, whose chief seat was at Halston Hall near Whittington. The best-known member of the family is 'Mad Jack' Mytton, who seems to have been mad in the true sense of the word, as well as in its 'sporting' connotation. Charles James Apperley ('Nimrod'), another Shropshire squire, who survived Mytton, wrote *Memoir of the Life of John Mytton*, describing the crazy exploits of this strange character. Later writers have also devoted more attention to his antics than they deserve, and he is the subject of an essay by Virginia Woolf, which shows a sympathetic insight into the possible cause of his unbalanced behaviour.

The road from Habberley to Shelve is more practicable for cars than it looks on the Ordnance Survey map. It climbs to the high

16 Weobley, Herefordshire

17 Staick House, Eardisland

moors of Pennerley with many twists and turns, from one of which there is a particularly fine backward view to Shrewsbury.

The moors are a good starting point for climbing the western flank of the Stiperstones. A road over the southern end of the Stiperstones, between Cranberry Rock and Nipston Rock, to Bridges, where there is a Youth Hostel, is convenient for climbing the eastern side, but wherever the starting point may be, the car must be left, and the journey made on foot.

This forbidding range of Ordovician rocks, veined with lead, has 20 or 30 foot outcrops of quartzite, perched along the top like gigantic ruins. The Stiperstones have an eerie aloofness which makes it easy to understand why so many legends are associated with them. Under lowering storm clouds they can look very intimidating, yet on a sunny day, walking along the 10-mile ridge from Scattered Rock to Nipstone, especially when the huge, juicy whimberries are in fruit, and the whole glorious panorama of this hill region can be seen, is a joyous enough experience to banish strange fancies.

The highest point (1,762 feet) is the Devil's Chair. It is said the Devil was making his way from Ireland with a load of stone to fill up Hell Gutter, but dropped them as he sat down to rest. Another tale tells that it was from here he threw the Lea Stone in the direction of Bishop's Castle. Yet another legend warns that if the Stiperstones sink into the earth, England will perish.

Other legends of the Stiperstones centre round 'Wild Edric', the Mercian thane who held lands in Shropshire and Herefordshire, and joined with his former enemies, the Welsh, against the advancing Normans, and kept the March in turmoil. He besieged and burnt Shrewsbury in 1069, but submitted to William the Conqueror the following year. He is said to have found a fairy bride when hunting over the Stiperstones, and she married him on condition he never mentioned her sisters. Some accounts say they were married in Westminster Abbey, in the presence of the Conqueror himself! They spent many happy years together until one day she provoked him by being unpunctual, and he exclaimed 'I suppose your sisters have kept you?' on which she vanished, and he shortly afterwards died of a broken heart. This linking of the old Celtic legend of the fairy bride with a Saxon thane has other versions, in which he and his

18 *The River Wye near Rhayader (Rhaeadre)*

bride were imprisoned under the Stiperstones, as a punishment for his submission to the Conqueror. It is said that he still rides with his soldiers over the Stiperstones; and that they will come again when war threatens England.

Shelve, consisting only of a church, a farm, and a few cottages, commands a superb view of the Stiperstones, boldly outlined against the sky. The small and beautifully-kept rubble church was rebuilt in 1839.

The innumerable place-names of this district ending in 'beach' are a corruption of 'batch', meaning an open space of ground near a river. The area has been mined for lead since the time of the Romans, and at Snailbeach a Roman pig of lead was found in 1851, stamped 'Imp. Hadrian Aug.', but the mines are all deserted now.

There is a road from Shelve to the southern end of Hope Valley, on the main road (A.488), near which is a rebuilt but entrancingly set church, below the road, and half-hidden in trees, with a flower-filled churchyard split in two by a stream, crossed by a little bridge across the ravine.

Continuing south between Forestry plantations on the east, and the curious, isolated Corndon Hill, crowned with cairns, rising 1,683 on the west, towards Lydham on a scantily sign-posted road, turn left at the cross-road where a sign-post points to 'Roveries' on the right, and with any luck you will reach More.

The Lord of More was Constable of the king's army, and held his manors under the obligation of contributing 200 footmen whenever any king of England led a hostile army into Wales; of leading the English van; and of carrying the Royal Standard in his own hand— onerous and dangerous duties which surely merited wide lands! Only the site of the castle remains, and the church has been re-built.

Linley Hall, which can be seen clearly from the road a mile north of More, is a Palladian stone mansion built in 1742 by Henry Joynes, surveyor of Kensington Palace. It was here that a very well-informed shepherd, asked for directions, withheld them until he had favoured me with his views on entry into the Common Market—and very sound, well-reasoned views they were! We parted in great amity.

Returning to the main road at Lydham, the A.488 runs south to Clun and Knighton, with the B.4384 turning off to Bishop's Castle, with its steep High Street running up to the handsome eighteenth-century town hall. Originally known as Lybury Castle, it came into the possession of the Bishops of Hereford in the time of Offa, under circumstances which are far from clear. One version says that Ethelbert, King of East Anglia, sought the hand of Offa's daughter, Elfrida, and was treacherously murdered by Offa, or by his queen. Another version says Ethelbert made love to Offa's wife; yet another version depicts Ethelbert as a Joseph accused by a Potiphar's wife. Whatever the truth, the unfortunate Offa had to do penance.

Miraculous cures were wrought at the grave of the Anglian king, who had been buried at Hereford, and among those who were healed was Egwin Shakehead, Saxon Lord of Lybury, who was cured of a palsy, and in gratitude, gave Lybury to the See. The manor covered 18,000 acres, and the Bishops of Hereford exercised a Lord Marcher's absolute jurisdiction until Henry VIII abolished the Marcher privileges, and under Elizabeth I, the bishop was forced to yield Lybury into the royal hands.

Once an important and busy place, returning two Members to Parliament, it was a municipal borough until 1967. Its castle has disappeared, and the site is occupied by an hotel dated 1719—naturally called The Castle Hotel. The eighteenth-century Market House has been pulled down, and the church has been rebuilt, with the exception of the Norman tower. Now rather 'off the beaten track', the pleasant, quiet town which wakes to bustling life on market days, has some attractive old houses, including the House on Crutches. The oldest inn is the Three Tuns, with a history dating back to 1642.

In 1837 Bishop's Castle still had a whipping post, and used it, and the story is told of a notorious local law-breaker whose character was belied by his venerable appearance. He was seen by the Victorian artist, Frederick Goodall, just before he was to be whipped—not for the first time. Struck by his saintly look, Goodall made a sketch of him in an attitude of prayer, which later, as the painting *Grace Before Meat*, was sold for a large sum of money, and engraved for sale to pious Victorians, to the amusement of the citizens of Bishop's Castle, and the gratification of the old reprobate.

There are numerous remains of castles and prehistoric camps in the neighbourhood, and at Lea, two miles east, is the ruined keep of one of the bishops' fortresses, and in a field close by, a large boulder, traditionally left there after the Devil removed it from his shoe when sitting in his chair on the Stiperstones, and threw it away—a pretty good throw, even for a supernatural being! The Lea Stone is also said to turn round when the clock strikes 13.

Returning north-east along the A.4383 to Lydham Heath, turn east along the A.489, following the course of the River Onny. A mile beyond the meeting of the East and West Onny is half-timbered Plowden Hall, which was built in the time of the great Elizabethan lawyer, Edmund Plowden, and still belongs to the same family. They were Roman Catholics, and the house has several secret hiding places. In the chapel is a brass to Humphrey Plowden and his family in Tudor costume. One of the family chaplains, Thomas Faulkner, was born in 1707, educated as a Presbyterian, and qualified as a doctor. He became a ship's surgeon, but fell ill and was put ashore at Buenos Aires. He was cared for by the Jesuits, became a Roman Catholic and later joined the Society of Jesus. He spent nearly 40 years as a missionary to South American tribes, but when the Jesuits were expelled from South America, he returned to England, and finally settled at Plowden Hall, where he died in 1784.

There is some Norman work surviving in the church of Lybury North, two and a half miles to the south-west of Plowden, including the entrance arch to the fourteenth-century Plowden chapel, which is said to have been founded by Roger Plowden, a crusader, as a thanksgiving for his safe return after being taken prisoner at the siege of Acre. It is a dark little chapel, contrasting with the sunny seventeenth-century Walcot chapel, which has prayer books embossed with the name of the first Lord Clive. The room over the Walcot chapel was formerly used as a school. Some of the pews in the nave still have the links and staples with which the worshippers fastened themselves in. The bell-frame is ornamented with dragons, and the fortress-like tower dates from the thirteenth century.

Walcot Hall, less than a mile from the church, is a brick mansion in a splendid park with a large lake. It was built in 1763 by Sir William Chambers for the first Lord Clive. Returning yet again to the main road, roads turn off north at intervals: one to Asterton joins the Portway; another from Hordeley cuts north-east to join the A.49 at Marshbrook, and a third climbs the south-eastern shoulder of Long Mynd to Woolston. The A.489 continues beside the Onny, with the rock-strewn, heather-clad heights of Long Mynd on the north and the great woods of Plowden on the south, and joins the Ludlow Road near Wistanstow.

CHAPTER SEVEN

Around Ludlow

Ludlow is the epitome of all the Marcher towns, with the most important of the many great Border castles. It surpasses the others not only in size, but in its crowded record of chivalry, treachery and ferocious warfare, and it is the only English castle which has its own medieval romance surviving to the present day. It is a long, rambling story written in the thirteenth century around the very fluctuating fortunes of Fulke Fitzwarine, lord of the castle in the twelfth century, Marion de la Bruyère, and her unchivalrous lover, Arnold de Lisle.

Ludlow came into the possession of the Lacys of Ewyas soon after the Conquest, and much of the castle is their work. The great keep dates from the time of Henry I, and the outer ward is not later than the reign of Henry II. It is at its most spectacular approached from the west, but it looms so formidably above any approach road, I always feel wonder at the hardihood of those who attempted to besiege it, and marvel that they ever succeeded, yet at times its fortunes changed so rapidly that its lords hardly knew when they left its walls whether they would find it garrisoned by their own men or their enemies when they returned.

The castle was inhabited and kept in repair to a much later date than most Marcher castles, and was much prized by the House of York, into whose possession it came by marriage in the fifteenth century. The two little Princes, sons of Edward IV, lived there before their journey to London, to their mysterious death in the Tower, and Prince Arthur took his bride, Catherine of Aragon, there, and died in the north-west tower in 1502. After his death it became the chief centre for the Council of the Marches. Sir Philip Sydney and his sister, Mary, afterwards Countess of Pembroke, played there as children, when their father, Sir Henry Sidney, was Lord President of Wales and the Marches. Milton's *Masque of Comus* was first performed in the Great Hall on 29 September 1634, when John, Earl of Bridgwater, was Lord President, and his two sons and a daughter-in-law acted in it.

It is not known whether Milton ever went to Ludlow, and although the 'Song' of Sabrina, the water nymph from whom the River Severn derives its name, has a few lines descriptive of scenery, it might equally well refer to the Thames near Milton's early home at Horton:

> *By the rushy-fringèd bank,*
> *Where grows the willow and the osier dank,*
> *My sliding chariot stays,*
> *Thick set with agate, and the azurn sheen*
> *Of turkis blue, and emerald green;*
> *That in the channel strays;*
> *Whilst from off the waters fleet*
> *Thus I set my printless feet*
> *O'er the cowslip's velvet head,*
> *That bends not as I tread.*

The claim of Comus 'I know each bank and every alley green...' may well be merely poetic licence.

When the Council of Wales and the Marches was abolished in 1699, the castle was allowed to fall into ruin, but was saved from total decay by its sale to the Earls of Powis in 1811. A Shakespearean play is performed annually in the open air, within the castle walls, for a fortnight during the summer.

With all the splendour and interest of the castle the town is far from being completely overshadowed. The rich beauty of its half-timbered houses, the great parish church, and the air of opulent peace and contentment with which it presides over its beautiful surroundings, make it unforgettable.

Broad Street, with its many ancient houses, climbs up from Ludford Bridge, and under the sole remaining gateway through the old walls. Among the wealth of old buildings mention may be made of the Elizabethan house at the top of Broad Street, in which the upper storey projects on dragon-beams, anticipating the modern cantilever system; The Reader's House, combining the stone-work of the original Church House with Tudor timber and plasterwork and a magnificent Jacobean porch; the Feathers Hotel, one of the most elaborate timber and plaster buildings in England; the Angel Hotel, projecting on pillars over the pavement; the Rose and Crown, first licensed in the sixteenth century and, of course, the splendid parish church, dating largely from the fourteenth and fifteenth centuries, and a treasure house of carved choir stalls, stained glass dating from 1430, and magnificent monuments. Fortunately, admirable and detailed guides can be obtained.

Stanley Weyman, the historical novelist, who enjoyed enormous popularity in his day, and is still read, was born at 54, Broad Street in 1855, and described it in a novel, *The New Rector* (1891), which gives a perfect description of life in Ludlow a century ago. Another Victorian, the children's writer, Mrs Molesworth, also made Ludlow the setting for *The Cuckoo Clock*, and for some of the scenes in *A Christmas Child*, published in 1880.

Set almost exactly in the centre of the Welsh Border, at the meeting place of many roads, Ludlow is inevitably a favourite touring centre, but has managed to avoid the cruder manifestations of popularity. Two of the Shropshire houses which are open to the public during the summer months are within easy reach : Elizabethan Whitton Court, four miles to the east, and The White House, Aston Munslow, nine and a half miles north.

It is strange that the beguiling Shropshire scenery inspired two writers so obsessed with death and decay and unrequited love as Mary Webb and A. E. Housman. Although Housman lies in the churchyard of Ludlow, he was not even the 'Shropshire Lad' Chesterton called him, but there is no denying that the district for which Ludlow is the centre has been given an almost other-worldly charm for many visitors, through his poems.

His most fervent admirers can hardly expect to find all his descriptions accurate, since he has himself revealed that some of his topographical details were purely imaginary. He was born at Bromsgrove, in Worcestershire, and Shropshire was on the western horizon 'which made me feel romantic about it', and he had not realized that 'the faithful would be making pilgrimages to these holy places'. One of his outstanding mistakes was his reference to Hughley steeple. After visiting Wenlock Edge in 1896, and realizing that the church had only a small, half-timbered bell-cote, he wrote to his brother Laurence: '...as I had already composed the poem and could not invent another name that sounded so nice, I could only deplore that the church at Hughley should follow the bad example of the Church at Bron, which persists in standing on a plain after Matthew Arnold has said that it stands among mountains'.

In connection with a book I wrote about Worcestershire, Laurence Housman was kind enough to give me some interesting information, much of which was later included in his *Memoir* of his brother. *Bredon Hill*, dated 1891, was the earliest of the poems which had place-names attached to them, and was originally the Worcestershire Bredon, not Shropshire, and the line 'Tis time I think, by Wenlock town' had 'Stourbridge town' in the first draft. Laurence thought that it was greater beauty of sound which decided the change to Shropshire, but there can be no possible doubt that Housman succeeded in capturing the scenery of the Shropshire hills in a way few more accurate writers have succeeded in doing, which more than justifies a 'pilgrimage' to the Housman Country, which is also of great interest in its own right.

The B.4365 to Wenlock Edge turns off the A.49 and runs through the lovely Corve Valley, passing close to Stanton Lacy, with its black and white cottages roofed with thatch or mellow tiles, its flower-filled gardens and its orchards. The church has a round-headed Saxon doorway, with a cross over it—one of the few known examples of Saxon sculpture. In the churchyard is a stone dated 1760 to Thomas Davies of Langley (a village a mile to the north which should not be confused with the more famous Langley near Acton Burnell). The epitaph reads:

> *Good natur'd, generous, bold and free*
> *He always was in company.*
> *He loved his bottle and his Friend*
> *Which brought on soon his latter end.*

Continuing north through Culmington, it is worth turning aside to see its church, on the banks of the Corve with much beautiful woodwork, including a fifteenth-century screen delicately carved, and a cornice of fan-like leaves crowned by Tudor roses. After Culmington, the road moves further from the river and nearer to the long limestone ridge of Wenlock Edge, joining the B.4368 at Pedlar's Rest, and turning right past the site of Corfham Castle, which was given by Henry II to Walter Clifford, father of Fair Rosamund, as 'hush money'.

Diddlebury is dominated by a church with much Saxon and Norman work. Thomas Baldwin, who is buried in the church, was a custodian of Mary, Queen of Scots, became implicated in plots on her behalf, and was imprisoned in the Tower of London. His epitaph suggests he had an adventurous life, for it records his escape from 'the sea, the sword and the cruel tower'.

A road from Diddlebury, winding north-east to Tugbury, gives access along a lane to the little Norman church of Heath—so appealing in its simplicity and its loneliness, in the centre of a field. It has no tower or belfry, but is a perfect example of a primitive Norman parish church with seventeenth-century pews and pulpit with their original crude carving and iron hinges, and a reader's desk with traces of chains which once fastened the Bible and prayer book to it: altogether a gem worth seeking out.

The gabled Swan and Crown at Munslow was the old Hundred House of Stottesden, where the Courts Leet were held. The church has Norman and medieval work, and a doorstep which includes a large brick from the Great Wall of China, brought to Munslow in 1884. A brass in memory of Richard Baldwin of Munslow, dated 1689, was restored in 1938 by the Shropshire Archaeological Society 'as a record that Stanley Baldwin, Earl Baldwin of Bewdley, K.G., is descended from the same family'. The White House, at Aston Munslow, has already been mentioned as one of those open to the public during the summer.

Munslow was the seat of the Littletons, one of whom, Edward Littleton, born in 1589, succeeded his father as Chief Justice for North Wales, and later became Chief Justice of England, and Keeper of the Great Seal. He proved to be a veritable 'Vicar of Bray' in his turn-coat propensities. He died at Oxford in 1645. Littleton's private life was irreproachable and as a judge he was incorruptible. Clarendon testified he was 'notorious for his courage which in his youth he had manifested with his sword', which makes his political instability inexplicable.

At Beambridge, where the Corve comes close again, the main road continues through Shipton, where the great Elizabethan manor house, with its stone-walled garden and medieval dovecote, is open to the public on Thursday afternoons in summer. The little church nearby has many memorials of the Mytton family.

Much Wenlock, midway between Shrewsbury and Bridgnorth on the A.458, is superbly situated, looking south to the Clee Hills, south-west along Wenlock Edge, and north to the Wrekin. The great, isolated hill, rising so steeply from the plain, is the natural landmark of the county, and so dear to Shropshire folk that whenever they gather together, anywhere in the world, the toast is always 'To all friends round the Wrekin'.

A nunnery was founded at Much Wenlock by St Milburga in the seventh century, but was destroyed by the Danes *c.* 896. It was restored by Earl Leofric and Lady Godiva as a college for secular canons, demolished after the Conquest, and re-founded as a Cluniac Priory by Roger de Montgomery in 1080. A succession of able Priors laboured to increase the importance of the Priory, and to advance the interests of the town, for which they procured many royal charters and privileges.

The ruins of the Priory date chiefly from the twelfth century; they are now in the care of the Department of the Environment, and are open all the year round. The Prior's Lodging, which Nicholas Pesvner describes 'as one of the finest examples of domestic architecture in England about the year 1500', and which is lovingly depicted by Henry James in *Portraits of Palaces*, is now a private house, and not open to the public.

The peaceful little town, so redolent of the past, has much Tudor architecture, with a half-timbered Guildhall which is picturesque without and splendidly panelled within. It houses a collection of carved oak furniture. The old stocks are mounted on a wheeled platform, which enabled them to be dragged round the town when in use.

Much Wenlock celebrated the Quincentenary of its Charter of

Incorporation in 1968. Sadly, although Edward IV's charter incorporated the town 'for ever', under the reorganization of local administration in 1966, the Borough of Wenlock ceased to exist. It became a Rural Borough—the first of its kind to be established in England. As part of the celebrations, a booklet was compiled giving many details of the history of the town since the granting of the charter.

The Wenlock Olympian Society was founded by a local doctor, William Penny Brookes, in 1850. By 1860 the games were open to the whole country, and Dr Brookes played a considerable part in the foundation of the International Olympic Games, although, of course, it was Baron Pierre de Coubertin who was the leading spirit of the modern revival in 1896, a year after Dr Brookes's death. It was the tireless work of Dr Brookes for athletics which resulted in a Government grant to schools for physical training. There is a memorial to him in the nave of the parish church, which also has a simple epitaph which lingers in the memory, to a boy of 16 who was 'His grandmother's friend'.

The road (B.4371) back to Ludlow runs along the crest of Wenlock Edge, that lovely, 16-mile ridge of the distinctive Wenlock limestone, where the infinite variety of delicate colouring of the opening buds of spring changes to white with the blossoming of hawthorn, cherry, guelder roses and rowan, before changing to the more uniform green of summer, and the blaze of scarlet and gold in autumn. These woods are alive with bird-song and are known to naturalists as a favourite haunt of green woodpeckers.

But first there are nearly two miles of limestone quarries to be passed, some abandoned, but some still working and shrouding trees and hedges in a uniform grey nearly to Major's Leap, a crag from which the royalist Major Thomas Sammwood of Wilderhope Manor leaped when carrying secret despatches for the King, to escape the pursuit of the Roundheads. The horse was killed, but the Major was saved by a tree growing out of the side of the rock, and finished his journey on foot.

Although Wenlock Edge never quite reaches 1,000 feet in height, it commands a wonderfully wide and varied panorama over Ape Vale, at its loveliest in spring with its snowdrops, primroses and wild daffodils, and the great swathes of bluebells which succeed them, to the Shropshire hills, backed by the Welsh mountains which are sometimes stark against the sky, but more often swathed in the delicious misty blue only distance can give. Northward over the foothills lies the flatter country between the lazy loops of the Severn and the hills, criss-crossed by streams, and country roads bordered by the Shropshire hedges, which are broader and thicker at the bottom than is usual in other English counties, with tops close clipped to a rounded contour.

A road to the right drops down to Hughley. The church has an exceptionally beautiful fifteenth-century chancel screen, perhaps the finest in all Shropshire, carved with grapes, flowers and birds.

Farther along the B.4371 is the viewpoint of Ippikins Rock, associated with a legend reminiscent of Ali Baba. It is said an outlawed knight lived in a cave with his robber band and their ill-gotten gains, but one day a landslip blocked the mouth of the cave, and buried them and their treasure. The outlawed knight, with a gold chain round his neck, haunts the rock, but if you are wise, you will not recite the magic words which would summon him, for if you do, he will throw you over the cliff to your death.

A mile farther is the village of Easthope, with an Elizabethan manor-house resembling Wilderhope. The church was attractively restored after a fire in 1923. It still has an hour-glass on a bracket, dated 1662, beside the pulpit. Under one of the yews in the churchyard are the reputed graves of two monks of Wenlock who, whilst staying in the half-timbered farm near the church are said to have quarrelled and killed each other. Their ghosts still haunt the place.

About two miles to the south-west is Wilderhope Manor, built in 1586, with fine plaster ceilings added in the following century. It is now the property of the National Trust, but it is leased to the Youth Hostel Association, and is only open in summer on Wednesday afternoons. Set in deep woods, it is by no means easy to find, and there is no road suitable for cars.

The B.4371 leaves the ridge shortly after leaving Easthope, for Longville-in-the-Dale, and runs through Ape Dale to Hope Bowdler and Church Stretton, with innumerable by-ways to the triangle between the Severn and the Hills already mentioned, of which it is only possible to echo Defoe: 'Indeed, this part of the county, and all the county of Salop is fill'd with fine seats of the nobility and gentry, too many so much as to give a list of, and much less to describe', although a mere handful of the most interesting may be mentioned.

Langley Chapel is an almost untouched Puritan church with the date 1601 on its roof timbers, high box pews for the gentry and their tenant farmers, and benches for the labourers and servants. The communion table is set well away from the wall, in accordance with Puritan practice, but instead of the long table round which Puritan communicants usually sat, there were kneeling desks and ledges fixed on three sides, of which two benches remain. It is a sad reflection on the growth of vandalism that this delightful chapel, so remote, and so charged with the atmosphere of the past, had to be closed owing to the theft of one of the furnishings, but it is now open again on Sunday afternoons. Close to the chapel is the gatehouse and moated site of Langley Manor House, home of the Lee family until 1660.

North of Langley is Acton Burnell, with the church and castle built by Robert Burnell, Bishop of Bath and Wells, the trusted friend and chancellor of Edward I. It was he who built the Bishop's Palace at Wells, and although his private life was scandalous and he is credited with being covetous, he played a large part in introducing reforms. It is no longer inhabited, but is in a better state of preservation than many Border castles. Among the memorials in the church is a canopied monument to Sir Richard Lee, who died in 1591, with his effigy and those of his wife, three sons and nine daughters, of which an endearing feature is a tiny dog peeping out from Sir Richard's empty gauntlet as it lies beside him.

Still farther north of Acton Burnell is the famous half-timbered Elizabethan Pitchford Hall, seat of the Ottleys for over 300 years. It can be seen through the lodge-gate or from the churchyard, but is not open to the public. The church is full of interest, with memorials to the Ottleys and a striking wooden effigy of Sir John de Pitchford, a thirteenth-century owner of the manor. The figure is clad in chain armour and surcoat, with a partly drawn sword, and the lion on which his feet rest is nibbling the end of the scabbard. The remarkable wooden tomb on which it rests is seven feet long, and is decorated with trefoil-headed arches, each containing a shield of arms suspended by a strap.

South-west of Acton Burnell along the line of the Roman road is Causeway Wood, with the Devil's Wood and Causeway where for over 500 yards the surface is paved with large blocks of stone to a width of 14 feet. It is almost needless to say that, according to Shropshire folklore, the Causeway was the work of the Devil!

Almost directly south, as the crow flies, is Plaish, reached by deep lanes reminiscent of Devon. Plaish Hall, which Pevsner and other authorities consider the most important of its date in Shropshire, can be glimpsed from the lane, and can be visited on Sunday afternoons during the summer. The house was begun by Sir William Leighton, Chief Justice of North Wales, and a member of the Council of the Marches during the reign of Elizabeth I. Among a number of stories associated with Plaish Hall is one of a murder, of which the bloodstains cannot be washed away; and another of a gathering of disreputable clergy, who played cards on a Sunday and were visited by the devil in person. Lord Chief Justice Leighton is buried in Cardington church.

There are roads from Cardington to Longville-in-the-Dale crossing Wenlock Edge to rejoin the B.4378 or by way of Rushbury to Beambridge, and so back to Ludlow.

There are various ways of getting to Clun from Ludlow, but doubtless the Housman enthusiasts will prefer to make for Clungenford, which stands at a cross-roads, with its church beside the winding River Clun and a large circular tumulus close by. There are several fine old houses in the neighbourhood.

The sturdy Norman keep of Hopton Castle is only a mile and a half to the west, on low-lying ground beside a stream. The small garrison of Parliamentarians held out valiantly when it was besieged in 1644, refusing quarter when it was offered, with the result that when it was taken, 29 of the 33 men were executed by the Royalists —a horrifying deed which might well alienate sympathy for the Royalist cause, were it not that this barbaric custom was practised also by victorious Parliamentarians.

The B.4367 runs directly north from Clungenford through the

pastoral valley of the Clun to join the B.4369 to Aston-on-Clun, with its curiously named 'Kangeroo Inn', neighboured by a stone Round House. At the cross-roads is a large poplar tree, which is decorated with flags annually on 29 May. They are left there until the following year, to commemorate the marriage of a lady born in 1712 at Aston House, who left a bequest to the poor. Here the B.4369 runs to Onibury; on the east, the B.4368 runs to Craven Arms, and there is a lane north to Hopesay, with a Norman church neighboured by prehistoric earthworks, in the shelter of Hopesay Hill, which belongs to the National Trust.

West from Aston-on-Clun the B.4368 runs direct to Clunton and Clun, with a short detour to Clunbury on the south bank of the Clun. The nave of Clunbury Church is Norman.

In the years before the 1939-45 war, a doctor and his wife settled in Clunbury and grew to know and love the district and its people. *An Idler on the Shropshire Borders*, by Ida Gandy, is a distillation of these years, giving an insight into country life as it really is, and not as novelists imagine it, with acute observations of the flora and fauna. It is a perfect introduction to Clun Forest.

Clun is set at the meeting of many roads and trackways, with the A.488 running north to Bishop's Castle and south to Knighton through New Invention—one of those odd names on the map which prick the imagination.

The town spreads over the banks of the river, which is crossed by an attractive but very narrow medieval bridge, with projecting angled piers to afford refuge to pedestrians, who had to keep a sharp eye open for the horse-drawn traffic, giving rise to the local saying 'Whoever crosses Clun Bridge comes home sharper than he went'.

The Norman keep and great earthworks are seen to the best advantage from the north-west. Originally built by Robert Say, a follower of Earl Roger de Montgomery, it was one of the earliest Norman castles along the Border, consisting of a motte and bailey; the present castle was built in the twelfth century. The enormous stone keep was adapted to the site by a curious projection into the ditch.

The Says of Clun seem to have left it to their neighbours of Wigmore to overrun the Welsh district of Maelienydd, to the west

19 *John Abel's screen, Abbey Dore*

of Clun Forest, but that did not save them from constant warfare. In 1142, Helias, third of the line, killed the Welsh Princes, Hywel and Cadwgan, and in 1195, Llywelyn the Great and his ally, Richard, Earl of Pembroke, burned Clun during their campaign against King John.

Clun is sometimes said to have been the original of the 'Garde Doloureuse' in *The Betrothed*, but although Scott stayed at the Buffalo Inn when gathering material for the novel, there are other equally plausible claimants for this honour—one of them is Painscastle in Radnorshire—and it appears likely that Scott had no particular castle in mind.

A road winds uphill from the castle to the church with its massive Norman tower capped by an odd, truncated pyramidal roof. It was occupied by Parliamentarians during the Civil War, and partly burnt in a battle with the Royalists. After the Restoration, Charles II ordered a national collection to pay for repairs. There is a splendid nave roof, partly of Perpendicular work, and a still more striking roof in the north aisle, with the outspread wings of angels upholding the moulded timbers of the quatrefoiled roof. Three other angels look down on the altar from the fifteenth-century wooden canopy, under which the pyx was hung. The Jacobean pulpit has a tester.

The church is dedicated to St George, of whom there is a painting by an Abyssinian artist—a memorial to one of the Thesiger family, who was killed on active service in 1942. A memorial in the churchyard records the deaths of seven children of the same family between the ages of four and 24, all carried off by a putrid fever in three weeks in 1811.

A heraldic brass with a coat-of-arms held by two little men in smocks is a memorial to Sir Robert Howard, who died in 1655. He had a romantic attachment to Frances Coke, daughter of the Lady Elizabeth Hatton and her second husband, the formidable Lord Chief Justice Coke. Richard Barham tells a fantastic and demonstrably untrue story of Lady Elizabeth in *The Housewarming* in *The Ingoldsby Legends*, but the true story is scarcely less fantastic. The callous treatment Frances and her mother endured at the hands of Coke, and the tribulations of Frances and her devoted Sir Robert, are told by Laura Norsworthy in *The Lady of Bleeding Heart Yard*.

20 *The River Wye at Hereford*

Another of the Howard family, Henry, Earl of Northampton, founded Clun Almshouses in 1614. They make a delightful group of stone cottages and a chapel, set around a quadrangle enclosing a garden.

Clun is the 'capital' of the Forest of Clun, and its ecclesiastical parish was once of immense size—16 miles from east to west, and 10 from north to south, which gave rise to a saying:

Clydach, Clyro and Clun,
Three largest parishes under the sun.

Some later variations were far from complimentary, but are now largely forgotten since Housman crystallized them into the perfect couplet:

Clunton and Clunbury, Clungunford and Clun
Are the quietest places under the sun.

South-west of the main ranges of the Shropshire Hills, and separated from them by the valleys of the Camlad (the only river which runs from England into Wales) and the Onny, Clun Forest covers about 17,000 acres and has some of the most memorable scenery of the Welsh Border. It is a wild and lonely region, thrusting westward deep into the even wilder and lonelier Kerry Hills of Montgomeryshire. It must have been a formidable barrier in earlier centuries, although even here the indomitable Mercians who constructed Offa's Dyke carried it right across the heights, and the Marcher Lords struggled desperately to extend their lordships—not always successfully.

Much of the area is still more Welsh than English, with a lilting accent in the speech of its people, and many place-names are of purely Celtic origin, especially in the west. It was not until 1537 that the boundary was finally settled, and it became a part of Shropshire.

The Forestry Commission has carried out an enormous amount of afforestation, and whilst the great proportion devoted to conifers is to be deplored, it must be admitted that in Clun Forest they are restoring, rather than changing, its ancient characteristics, for there is evidence to show that it was densely wooded until the ever-growing demand for timber for ship-building, charcoal burning, and for the great half-timbered houses and cottages of Shropshire and Herefordshire, depleted the area during the Tudor period.

There are far-reaching views of the Shropshire hills and plain, and of the Welsh mountains, particularly from Badger Moor on Black Mountain, or Stoney Pound, in the south; along the line of Offa's Dyke as it crosses Craig Hill on the east; Two Crosses on the north; and not the least extensive and magnificent are the views from the main road between Clun and Kerry.

Few people are to be met with on these uplands, but they have long been the haunt of many wild birds, although some species are decreasing as afforestation is extended. This also curtails some of the age-old sheep runs, but there are still vast flocks of the local breeds of the Clun, Radnor and Kerry sheep—the latter easily recognizable by their white faces and black markings around their eyes, which make them look absurd caricatures of women with too much make-up. There are also some of the hardy Welsh Black cattle.

The villages of the eastern foothills are most easily reached from Clun, and Mainstone, on the north, is only four and a half miles from Bishop's Castle, but has a more spectacular approach over the hills from Newcastle-under-Lyme. Mainstone lies in the valley of the little River Unk, with its church a mile away at Church Town in another valley. The simple little building has been so altered in seventeenth- and eighteenth-century restorations that little remains of the original Decorated work. The village is said to derive its name from a granite boulder weighing about 230 pounds, which can be seen there still. In former times the villagers would show their strength by heaving the stone above their heads and throwing it backwards over the left shoulder.

Betws-y-Crwyn, The Beata Domus, or Bede House of the Skins, on the south of Clun Forest, has a church standing over 1,300 feet above sea level—probably the highest church site in England. It is an appropriately sturdy building to resist the gales which can sweep across these uplands, and the Victorian restoration has preserved the roof, which is typical of the region, and the fine Late Perpendicular screen of Spanish chestnut. The names of the farmhouses of the district, known locally as 'Halls', are shown on the solid oak benches. The church possesses an interesting silver chalice, hall-marked 1665.

A seventeenth-century grave in the churchyard recalls the story of a travelling pedlar who collapsed and died (or was murdered) near Crossways. The neighbouring parishes showed a deplorable lack of Christian charity by arguing as to the responsibility for burying the stranger, but finally Betws-y-Crwyn gave him a resting place. By a belated return of 'bread cast upon the waters', some two centuries later, when the Clun Forest Enclosure Act of 1875 was passed, and parish boundaries were re-adjusted, Betws obtained several hundred additional acres on the northern boundary of the parish, on the evidence of the Cantlin Stone, which had been put on the spot where the pedlar died, with the inscription 'W.C. decsd here buried 1691 at Betvs'. This flat slab of limestone is inconspicuous, but is neighboured by a carved cross set up by Beriah Botfield, a Member of Parliament for Ludlow.

Beguildy is on the Radnorshire banks of the River Teme, which curves round the southern foot of Clun Forest. Beguildy Church is largely fourteenth century, apart from the tower which was rebuilt after it fell down in the late nineteenth century. The fifteenth-century screen, although much worn, is of good English design with some original colouring, and the old timber roof is of the typical Radnorshire open type with quatrefoil wind-braces.

Llanvair Waterdine, further down the river on the road to Knighton, is now in Shropshire. It can be reached by a trackway from Newcastle-under-Lyme giving glorious views before dropping down the wooded Cwm Collo. The remote and scattered village has a rebuilt church with parts of the old screen used to form the communion rail. It is a mass of carving of men, women, bunches of grapes, deer, pigs, rabbits, dogs and other beasts, including a lion and a dragon. It also bears a Welsh inscription which baffled translation for many years, but is now believed to mean 'Sir Matthew and Meyric Pichgar of Clun set it (the rood-screen) for ten pounds together'. A Sir Matthew was incumbent in 1485-1520. The grave of a gypsy in the churchyard has a Romany inscription.

The B.4355 continues south-east beside the Teme to Knighton, and from there a number of different roads lead back to Clun or Ludlow.

The B.4368 across the Clun Forest to Newtown in Montgomeryshire follows the course of the River Clun almost to its source in the Kerry Hills. Just before reaching Newcastle-under-Lyme, impressive stretches of Offa's Dyke can be seen on either side. Newcastle-under-Lyme itself is undistinguished, but it is guarded by hills on either side the Folly Brook, each of which is crowned with a prehistoric camp. Crossing the River Clun, the road branches right to Whitcott Keysett, which has a menhir eight feet high beside the river, and on to Mainstone; the B.4368 continues beside the Clun, past Hall-of-the-Forest (now a farm), where Sir Robert Howard took Frances Coke for safety, to the lonely, wind-swept Anchor Inn. Beyond the inn the road crosses a hollow of heather and bog-pools into Wales and climbs the summit-ridge, here called Kerry Pole, on a steep lane which cuts out the main road winding around a plantation of trees. At Glan-Mule cross-roads there is a choice between the A.489 road to Newtown, or the longer road to Abermule at the confluence of the River Mule with the Severn.

The Newtown road runs through Kerry (Ceri), a lonely little place in the hills which had its great moment of excitement in 1176, when a bitter and unseemly dispute broke out over the consecration of the church. The Bishop of St Asaph claimed it was within his diocese, and Giraldus Cambrensis, Archdeacon of Brecon, was equally convinced it was within the diocese of St David's. Each excommunicated the other on the spot, but Giraldus won handsomely, for he had arrived first and taken possession of the church, which enabled him to ring a triplet of bells to establish an effective rite of excommunication, and the Bishop had to retire from the contest.

CHAPTER EIGHT

The Radnorshire Border

Radnor Forest and the Valleys of the Teme, Lugg and Arrow

The nearest towns to Radnor Forest are Knighton, on the River Teme, Presteigne, on the River Lugg, or Kington on the River Arrow on the east, and Llandrindod Wells, in the Valley of the Ithon on the south-west.

Approaching from England, Bromfield or Ludlow are nearest to Knighton by the A.4113 to Leintwardine, a Herefordshire village believed to be on the site of the Roman city of *Bravinium*. Leintwardine church stands on the Roman earthworks, and Roman tiles and bricks have been discovered under the chancel.

The main street drops steeply down to the old stone bridge over the River Teme. The large church, with its massive battlemented tower, dates from various periods, and has some splendid woodwork, including a side screen with fifteenth-century tracery, and six stalls of the same period, said to have been brought from Wigmore Abbey.

The road continues along the valley of the Teme to Brampton Bryan, an attractive place with a village green, which took its name from Bryan de Brampton, a thirteenth-century owner. An effigy in the church is said to be that of Margaret, the last of the Bramptons, whose marriage in 1309 to Sir Robert Harley brought him to the village. The fourteenth-century gatehouse in the park of the newer Hall is all that is left of the castle defended so valiantly by Lady Brilliana Harley. She refused to surrender to the Royalists in the absence of her Parliamentarian husband, but the strain of the siege was too much for her, and she died shortly afterwards.

Over 200 of her letters were published in the nineteenth century by the Camden Society. Many of them were written at Brampton Bryan.

The church was destroyed at the same time as the castle, and was rebuilt in 1656 by her widower. Lady Brilliana, her husband, their eldest son, Sir Edward, their grandson, the first Earl of Oxford, and other members of the family are buried in the church.

North of Brampton Bryan is the wooded Coxall Knoll, with the remains of a fortified prehistoric camp, among the numerous places where tradition says Caradog made his last stand against the Romans. Farther up the valley of the Teme, the boundary between Shropshire and Wales is crossed and re-crossed several times before reaching Knighton.

This Radnorshire market town is properly Trefyclawdd, The Town on the Dyke, for it is actually built on Offa's Dyke. Knighton became the headquarters of the Offa's Dyke Association at its foundation, and also of the Trefyclawdd '1970' Society, a local body which raised the money to purchase and 'landscape' a stretch of the Dyke, to provide an appropriate setting for the opening ceremony of the Long-distance Path.

The Saxons are credited with the first settlement at Knighton, but this was overrun by the Welsh in 1052. The Normans came soon after 1066, and built a castle—probably on the mound east of the town at Bryn-y-Castell. Knighton stands 700 feet above sea level, in a bowl of higher hills, and there are steep, narrow streets with some attractive buildings still remaining in the upper part of the town, known as 'The Narrows', although all too much rebuilding has taken place.

The town was granted to the Mortimers by Henry III, and in 1460 passed with all the other Mortimer possessions, to Edward, Earl of March, afterwards Edward IV, when it became Crown property.

Knighton is fortunate enough to retain its railway station on the Central Wales line, just over the border in Shropshire. The railway links it to Craven Arms and Shrewsbury, and runs south-west to Llandrindod Wells and Swansea.

Knucklas, three miles north-west of Knighton, can be reached by rail or road. It is the site of Knucklas Castle, romantically perched on a high, lonely hill. It was long a stronghold of the Mortimers, but the site was probably occupied in prehistoric times, and tradition connects it with Arthurian legends, asserting that from this spot

Arthur was married to Guinevere, daughter of Cogfran Gawr, the giant who lived here.

Vavasour Powell, one of the most popular of the early Nonconformist preachers, was born at Knucklas in 1617. He was a man of strong convictions who was constantly in trouble with the authorities. He died in the Fleet Prison in 1670, and was buried in Bunhill Fields.

The railway curves through a valley bordered by high hills to Llangunllo Halt, which is at a considerable distance from Llangunllo village, with its rebuilt church, in the valley of the Lugg. It continues through numerous rocky cuttings to Llanbister Road Halt, which is even farther from Llanbister village. A hilly lane from the Halt winds north to the B.4356 from Llangunllo to Llanbister, high above the River Ithon, or the adventurous can struggle across a waste of scrubby gorse, unsignposted for many miles and with a barely discernible track in places, and down across the Camddwr, a tributary of the Ithon, and up the steep hill on which the church is placed—the reward of so much struggle, lovely in proportion and interesting in detail. It is mostly thirteenth-century work, sympathetically restored by W. D. Caroë in 1908. The fifteenth-century screen has some modern additions, and the pews have been adapted from the original Georgian box pews, but the pulpit and tester and the communion rails are untouched, and there is a perfect musician's gallery dating from 1716. There is a fine modern reredos behind the altar, and the unique addition of a modern baptistry. Llanbister is within a short distance of the A.483 road, already mentioned, which keeps company with the Ithon nearly to its source, as it runs north to Newtown, and south through Llandrindod Wells to its confluence with the River Wye. Although Llanbister is itself almost beyond the limit of the Border proper, those who have journeyed so far might well follow the road for the additional mile or two northward to Llananno, where one of the finest early sixteenth-century screens in Wales has been preserved in the tiny rebuilt church.

Radnor Forest, a compact, flat-topped hill block, seamed with delightful valleys, was for centuries a forest in the old meaning of an unenclosed space used only for hunting, but in recent years the Forestry Commission has striven to give the word its modern meaning, and great areas have been planted. There is still a good deal of open moorland, but the encroaching trees are inevitably affecting the wild life of the Forest—and even the human life, as lonely, derelict cottages testify.

The Radnor sheep, with speckled faces and legs, roam freely over the moorland heights, which are also the home of wild Welsh ponies, and the district has a great attraction for pony-trekkers. There are good roads ringing Radnor Forest, but unlike Clun Forest, it has no roads crossing the summit, apart from the new tracks laid down by the Forestry Commission, and it can only be explored on foot or on horse-back. There is no place along the Border more exhilarating in good weather, or more dangerous in misty weather. It is easy to get lost away from the main tracks, and the marshy bogs and sudden rocky precipices can be death traps.

Leaving Knighton by the A.488, the valley of the Lugg is crossed at Monaughty, where a fine Tudor house is now a farm, to Bleddfa, beautifully situated at the northern edge of Radnor Forest. The church crowns a prehistoric mound beside the main road. The stone-work is chiefly thirteenth century, with a weather-boarded belfry. There is a fourteenth-century roof with king-posts and queen-posts and seventeenth-century communion rails. Llanfihangel Rhydieithon church, on the north-west of the Forest, was entirely rebuilt in 1891 and everything of interest removed, except for the fourteenth-century font bowl.

At Pen-y-bont, on the River Eithon, the A.488 meets the A.44 from Rhayader to Kington. Although it is at the meeting of roads, and has a railway station a mile away, there is little hint now of its importance in previous centuries. The Severn Arms was a famous coaching inn under its former name of The Fleece, the Radnorshire Agricultural Society and a Radnorshire Bible Society held their meetings at Pen-y-bont for many years, and the Radnorshire Bank was instituted there. It was also the headquarters of the county police for a time in the nineteenth century. The Pen-y-bont Races had a longer continuous history than any others in the county, and were described as 'old' in 1850.

Turning south-west along the A.44, Llandegly (Llandeglau) is reached. The church, largely rebuilt in the nineteenth century, is dedicated to St Tegla, and, it is said, 'very curious customs' were practised at St Tegla's well in the Middle Ages, by sufferers hoping for a cure.

The Pales, a stone building with a thatched roof and the date 1745, is the oldest meeting house in Wales of the Society of Friends. It preserves some of the original furniture.

The Llandegly rocks, which rise 1,400 feet south of the village, give a magnificent view of Radnor Forest.

The A.44 is joined at Forest Inn by the A.481 from Builth Wells, which passes close to the Feddw Circle, one of the largest in Wales. Forest Inn is one of the starting points for the quaintly named waterfall, Water-break-its-neck, which lies in a wooded valley and drops precipitously some 70 or 80 feet into a dark chasm—a mere trickle in dry weather, but a torrent after rain. There is a path down the side of the stream to rejoin the main road, which runs through uncultivated country. Less than a mile from Forest Inn it passes the church of Llanfihangel Nant Melan, in a ring of yew trees believed to mark the line of a stone circle, with the little Summergill Brook flowing below. It was rebuilt in 1846, but retains memorials to the family of Squire Butts, a well-known Master of the only pack of fox-hounds in Radnorshire in the eighteenth century. Opposite the church is an old Welsh 'longhouse'. There is a breezy camping site 1,300 feet up on Llyn Heilyn, which commands fine views.

New Radnor, which was a Borough from the time of Elizabeth I until 1886, and the county town, is now a village. The castle built by the Normans and sacked by Owain Glyn Dŵr was finally destroyed in the Civil War, but the church was wantonly pulled down in 1843 and replaced by the uninteresting building of today. New Radnor is laid out on a simple chequerboard pattern which has been attributed to the Saxon Earl Harold, but is more likely to date from the thirteenth century. The conspicuous memorial in the centre of the village was set up in memory of Sir George Cornewall Lewis, of Harpton Court, the Whig statesman and scholar so much admired by Walter Bagehot. He was a member of one of the oldest families in Radnorshire, who had their seat at Harpton Court, about a mile and a half south-east of New Radnor.

It was from New Radnor that Archbishop Baldwin and Giraldus

Cambrensis began their preaching tour of Wales. They were entertained there by Rhys ap Gruffydd, Prince of South Wales, a kinsman of Giraldus, who was in possession of the castle in 1188. They made their way to Cruker Castle, sometimes wrongly identified as that of Old Radnor, but which was Crug Eryr (*Castrum Crukeri*), the site of which is marked by a mound and enclosure, a mile beyond Forest Inn. It is one of the best examples in the country of a Norman motte and bailey.

Old Radnor, two and a half miles from New Radnor, has a church on an outcrop of rock, and very little else, but it is of such interest that it should not be missed. Even the splendid Perpendicular oak screen is less important than its font, which is probably the earliest existing font in Britain. It was made out of a megalithic stone, and has been used as a font since the eighth century. The organ case dates from about 1500, and is said to be the only one of its kind in existence. It is now fitted out with nineteenth-century pipes and mechanism. The carving on the screen is said to have been the work of a Gloucestershire School of carvers, and is a beautifully preserved sister screen to the mutilated screen in Cirencester Church. There is ancient glass, medieval choir stalls, an Easter sepulchre, and other interesting details, all of which are described in the guide to the church.

The church stands 840 feet above the sea level, and looks away over the level valley to the standing stones near Kinnerton. A mile eastward are the Stanner Rocks, known locally as the 'Devil's Garden', with many rare species of flowers. All Radnor Forest is noted for its wild flowers, in the valleys and on the hills.

The B.4372 branches off at New Radnor, and at Beggars Bush the B.4357 runs to Bridge End, where there is a bridge across the Lugg to Whitton and the B.4356 to Pilleth, where Owain Glyn Dŵr took Sir Edmund Mortimer prisoner in 1402. According to tradition, 1,100 of Mortimer's army were killed as they were driven down Bryn Glas (Pilleth Hill), and many bones were uncovered by ploughing, until a clump of trees was planted to mark the site. At Monaughty crossroads, the A.488 from Knighton is rejoined, having completed the circuit of the Forest.

Roads from Old Radnor lead to Kington or Presteigne. The parting of the routes is at Walton, on the Hindwell Brook, close to the

Hereford boundary. Wordsworth stayed there with relatives in an old farmhouse beside the Hindwell Pool.

Presteigne (Llanandras) is the smallest county and assize town in Wales or England, yet it is the third largest town in the sparsely populated county of Radnorshire. The assizes have been held there for over 400 years, and its history spans more than 10 eventful centuries.

There is a generally accepted tradition that Caradog commanded the camp of the Ordovices on the neighbouring Wapley Hill, and set out from there for his fateful battle with the Romans. Offa built his Dyke three miles west of Presteigne, which was founded by the Saxons, who gave the town its name, believed to be originally Pres-themede (*preosta haemed*) the household of priests. The name probably referred to the church, which served a wide area. The Welsh name is derived from the dedication of the church to St Andrew.

The Saxon Edward the Confessor gave the manor to Richard Fitz Scrob, the Norman founder of Richard's Castle. It eventually came into the possession of the Mortimers of Wigmore. It was ravaged many times in the Welsh wars, and during the Wars of the Roses the hills and woods around the town became so infested with lawless men that Bishop Roland Lee, President of the Council of the Marches, came there in 1535 to lie 'among the thickest of the thieves'. He is said to have hanged 5,000 malefactors along the Border before peace and order were finally restored. The following year, the Act of Union created the new county of Radnorshire, with New Radnor as the shire town. Presteigne became the capital of the county after the Civil Wars, when the Great Sessions were transferred from New Radnor.

Presteigne was strongly royalist in the Civil War. Charles I, who had had a hunting lodge nearby (traditionally at Barland), knew the district well, and came there twice after his defeat at Naseby in 1645. On the second occasion the army crossed the bridge over the River Lugg into the town after being on the march from 6 a.m. to midnight. No wonder J. R. Phillips says in *Memoirs of the Civil War in Wales* that 'they trudged wearily along the rough and uneven country roads'!

Presteigne is typical of the smaller Border towns, with a wide main street and numerous by-ways where beautiful old houses can be found. Its air of peaceful prosperity still has power to charm me, although it can never seem quite the same since the death of W. H. Howse, the kindly historian of Radnorshire. His knowledge of every facet of his beloved county's history, folklore, customs and natural history made any talk or walk with him a delight, and no-one who visits the district can fail to profit from his book *Radnorshire*, or the many guides he wrote for the local towns and churches.

His researches enabled him to confirm or disprove some of the accepted local traditions, and it especially pained his scholarly mind that writers on the Welsh Border country continued to give credence to the story that the Radnorshire Arms, built in 1616, was originally the home of the regicide John Bradshaw or his brother. It is due to his memory to make it clear that the regicide came from an old Cheshire family, and had no connection whatever with the John Bradshaw of Presteigne, who was an ardent royalist, and a member of a family which had settled in Presteigne in 1540.

George Borrow stayed at the Radnorshire Arms, and was told by the maidservant that Presteigne was neither in England nor Wales, but 'in Radnorshire'.

Presteigne's spacious parish church dates chiefly from the fourteenth and fifteenth centuries, but has traces of Saxon and Norman work. Its chief treasures are a tall silver flagon of 1692, and a magnificent early sixteenth-century Flemish tapestry, one of a set woven for Canterbury Cathedral, the remainder of which were sold to the authorities of the cathedral of Aix-en-Provence during the Commonwealth.

The rent of a field known as the Bell Meadow was left in 1565 for the curfew, which is still rung from the church tower, every evening, summer and winter, at eight o'clock.

It was in this church that 13 parsons gathered in the seventeenth century to exorcise the evil spirit of Black Vaughan of Hergest Court, near Kington, whose ghost haunted the neighbourhood. Carrying lighted candles, they summoned him to appear, but when his spirit did so, 12 of them fainted with fright. The thirteenth bravely carried on and eventually reduced the evil spirit to the size of a bluebottle fly. He caught and imprisoned it in a snuff-box, which was then buried under a large stone in Hergest Pool, and so the ghost was finally laid to rest.

Legend tells of a black hound associated with a local family, which roams the hills around Presteigne. In spite of the fact that Sir Arthur Conan Doyle himself, in his preface to *The Complete Long Stories of Sherlock Holmes*, says 'a remark by Fletcher Robinson ... that there was a spectral dog near his home on Dartmoor was the inception of the book (*The Hound of the Baskervilles*) but I should add that the plot and every word of the actual narrative was my own', it has been claimed that the Presteigne hound was used as the basis of the story!

The bridge over the River Lugg, at the foot of Broad Street, links Wales and England, and the line of division between Radnorshire and Herefordshire is shown on the bridge. It is an indication of Presteigne's claims as a centre for a wonderful variety of scenery in England and Wales, and no more delightful tours could be made than those to the Radnor Forest, the 'black and white' districts of Herefordshire, the Shropshire Highlands, the central Wye Valley and many beautiful and interesting manor houses on both sides of the Border. Among these, special mention may be made of Titley Court, once the home of Lady Greenly, extracts from whose *Diaries* have been published in the *Transactions* of the Woolhope Club. She spoke Welsh fluently, and was an enthusiastic supporter of eisteddfodau held in Brecon and Abergavenny. She was a valued member of the Llanover Circle, of which mention will be found in the chapter on the Usk Valley.

Wordsworth and Shelley once stayed at Eywood, the property of the Earl of Oxford, and Byron, who was charmed with the neighbourhood, took a lease of the Earl's other house, Kinsham Court, where later Florence Nightingale spent some of her childhood. Especially interesting is the perfect seventeenth-century house of The Rodd, home of Lord Rennell of Rodd, who tells the history of his house, and other manors of the Herefordshire March of Wales, in *Valley on the March*.

The return from Presteigne to Ludlow can be made by the B.4362 through Shobdon, which lies midway between the valleys of the Lugg and the Arrow. The church was rebuilt by Lord Bateman in the eighteenth century in 'Strawberry Hill Gothic', leaving only the thirteenth-century tower. The misguided peer removed the splendid Norman carvings by sculptors of the Herefordshire School of sculpture who were also responsible for Kilpeck Church, and re-erected them on a hill in his park, north of the village, where they have weathered badly. Drawings were made of them by G. R. Lewis when they were still in good condition. They were published in 1852, and show the variety and beauty of the carvings. Only the Norman font, with well-carved lions, was left in the church to show the age of its foundation. At Mortimer's Cross, near the monument commemorating the battle of 1461, the B.4362 crosses the A.4110, and there is a choice of roads back to Ludlow, or to Leominster and Hereford.

The A.4110 follows the line of a Roman road north to Aymestrey, a delightful village with a fine church in which there is a most delicately carved sixteenth-century screen. The road winds north from Aymestrey to Wigmore, one of the innumerable black and white villages for which Herefordshire is so famous. Wigmore Hall, at the south end of the village is particularly attractive.

Those who enjoy moralizing on the vanity of human ambition can enjoy themselves in almost any Border town, but in none more than in Wigmore, once the chief seat of the Mortimers, who played a leading part in the history of England, Wales and Ulster. They had a talent for extending their lands and prestige, but the male line died out, and Wigmore passed through the female line to the Dukes of York, and ended with the English kings, Edward IV and Richard III, whose lands were carried by Elizabeth of York to the first Tudor king, Henry VII.

Today the castle gateway and ruined keep are a mere fragment of the original fortress, of which a complex of mounds and ridges shows the expert the former extent. The remains of Wigmore Abbey, founded in 1179, are two miles north of the village, at Adforton. The church in which many of the Mortimers were buried has vanished, and its stones are to be found in a number of houses around. Part of the west end of the monastic buildings is preserved in Wigmore Grange farm-house, the remainder are lovely in decay.

All around Wigmore and Adforton is a tangle of lanes and wide stretches of woodlands too complicated to be described clearly, but easily found on a good map. Especially lovely are the walks through the ancient Forest of Deerfold, which was a sanctuary of the Lollards during the savage persecutions they endured. The famous Sir John Oldcastle found refuge at Chapel Farm for four years before he was discovered and martyred. The woods extend to the banks of the Lugg, with many ancient trees, and masses of wild flowers, including rare species. In the neighbourhood of Lingen there is the site of a motte and bailey castle, and the remains of Limebrook Priory, founded in 1189 by Robert de Lingen.

East of Wigmore are even more extensive woodlands, merging into Bringewood Chase, which stretches along the banks of the Teme at Downton, and eastward nearly to Ludlow. The wooded gorge at Downton owes much to the activities of Richard Payne Knight, M.P. for Ludlow, who spent much time and money in planting trees to enhance the view from Downton Castle, the 'Gothic' mansion he built high above the Teme. He died in 1824, and bequeathed his superb collection of coins and bronzes to the British Museum. These woods offer some of the loveliest walks and drives on the Border.

A shorter route back to Ludlow leaves Mortimer's Cross by the B.4362 to Cock Gate, where there is a turning to Croft Castle which, apart from a break of 170 years from 1750, has been the home of the Croft family since Domesday. The earliest parts of the present castle date from the fourteenth and fifteenth centuries, with 'Gothic' additions made between 1750 and 1760 by the Johnes family of Hafod. There are magnificent avenues of oak, beech and Spanish chestnut in the park. The property was acquired by the National Trust in 1957, and is open at advertised times during the summer. The estate includes Croft Ambrey, with its great Iron Age fort and spectacular views, and the Fishpool Valley. In the small parish church near the house are many memorials to the Croft family, and a magnificent tomb with the effigy of Sir Richard, wearing the armour in which he fought at Tewkesbury, and his wife.

Beyond Cock Gate the B.4362 joins the B.4361. Close to the county boundary is the village of Richard's Castle, with houses in Herefordshire and Shropshire.

Richard's Castle was a pre-Conquest Norman foundation, and so few stones remain that it would not be worth the struggle up the

steep path to see them, were they not neighboured by the old parish church, which is now used only for funerals, but is carefully preserved. There is a glorious view from the summit. The manor of Richard's Castle is still in the possession of the Salwey family, who held lands in Staffordshire in the reign of Henry III, and seized Richard's Castle in 1402. The seventeenth-century Court House, on the south-east of the village, has a dovecot and an old cider mill in the grounds. Ludlow is only three miles from Richard's Castle.

The most direct road from Ludlow to Leominster and Hereford, the A.49, runs south through the valley of the Teme as far as Brimfield, and the valley of the Lugg between Leominster and Hereford. This undulating countryside is less dramatic than the Shropshire hill country and the Welsh mountain regions, but has a charm all its own in its ordered, man-made beauty, with the bright colouring of the vivid red earth and the red and white Herefordshire cattle; the intense green of the pastures and trees, occasionally broken by great stretches of golden corn; the pear trees, grown for making perry, and the apple-orchards decked with pink-tinged blossom in Spring and rosy red apples in autumn—those apples which look so tempting, and are so bitter to the taste—fit only for the cider presses for which they are destined.

There is so much to see in Ludlow that Ludford, on the opposite bank of the Teme, is too often neglected, yet it is well worth exploring for its own sake, and for the splendid view, from Whitcliff, of Ludlow against its background of hills and mountains.

Ludford church has been much altered through the centuries, but there are still some traces of Norman work, the main fabric dating from the fourteenth and sixteenth centuries. There is a fine range of memorials. The earliest is a large brass of 1554 to William Foxe with his wife and 14 children. An altar tomb has an effigy of Sir Job Charlton, Speaker of the House of Commons, who entertained James II at Ludford House. He died in 1697, and his painted effigy depicts him with long hair, wearing a black skull cap and a scarlet gown. It was Sir Job Charlton who, having fallen out of favour with Charles II, had to resign to make way for Judge Jeffreys, although his appointment was afterwards restored.

There is a view from the churchyard of the gabled roofs of the almshouses, manor-house and mill. The Hospital of St Giles was founded in the time of Henry III, rebuilt in 1500, and given its present form by Sir Job Charlton in 1672.

Ludford House dates partly from the thirteenth century. It is a very large building, with the lower part of massive stone work, and the upper part of Tudor half-timbering. Over the porch is an oratory with a secret passage.

Beyond the almshouses is the former Bell Inn, now a private house, and farther down the road is the ancient flour mill, beside the river, looking away to the Clee Hills.

Farther down the valley of the Teme are the villages of Ashford Bowdler and Ashford Carbonel. Ashford Bowdler has a quaint old church with some small Norman windows 'restored' in 1853, on the steep west bank of the river.

Ashford Carbonel, on the east bank of the Teme, is reached by an ancient bridge, and has some attractive black and white houses, with the church on a hillside above, looking away to the Clee Hills on the north-east, and west to the Welsh border. The church contains much Norman work, and if the two small, plain round-headed Norman windows of the eleventh century and the beautiful vesica above are contemporary, they form one of the earliest examples of round and pointed arches associated together. Vesica windows, with their egg shape, are now extremely rare. They were employed frequently as an architectural feature and by early Christian artists, usually to enclose figures of Christ or the Virgin.

As the boundary of Herefordshire is crossed, the Teme turns east from the main road, and Brimfield is reached, with its over-restored church and its thatched and timbered cottages. It is the last village the road passes through on the way to Leominster, but fascinating places can be reached down the by-ways.

West of the road is Orleton with its black and white houses grouped around the meeting of four roads. The medieval church has a timber spire and porch. The lovely sixteenth-century Orleton Court was long the home of the Blount family with whom Pope was so friendly, but under the extraordinary will of the last male heir, it was left to Yale University. It seems probable the village was the birthplace of Adam de Orleton, although the *Dictionary of National*

Biography says he was probably born in Hereford. He championed the cause of Queen Eleanor and her paramour Mortimer against Edward II, and was charged with treason. He is said to have been the first English bishop to be brought before a lay court, and he challenged its jurisdiction, and eventually forced Edward II to abdicate. He was successively Bishop of Hereford, Worcester and Winchester, and was buried in Hereford Cathedral. Also born at Orleton, in 1869, was Sir Arthur Keysall Yapp, who was National Secretary of the Y.M.C.A. He entered the Association at the age of 21, and served it for over 50 years. It was he who introduced the Red Triangle as its symbol.

Middleton on the Hill, east of the road, is close to the Worcestershire border. It has a moated house dating from the sixteenth and seventeenth centuries, called Moor Abbey, from the days when it belonged to the monks of Leominster, and a simple little church which is chiefly Norman, with a tower dating from the thirteenth to the fifteenth centuries.

Half-way to Leominster, the road runs beside the eastern boundary of the great park of Berrington Hall, which was laid out by Capability Brown. The house was built of red sandstone for Thomas Harley by Henry Holland between 1778 and 1793, and remains almost unaltered, with elaborate plaster ceilings and splendid furniture. It now belongs to the National Trust. The house is so much enhanced by the beautiful setting that a suspicion of nepotism (Holland was a relative of Lancelot Brown by marriage) can be forgiven. Eye manor, another National Trust property, is a mile to the west. It was built in 1860 by a Barbados slave trader, Ferdinando Gorges, who had grown wealthy on that inhuman trade. It shows an artistic taste which seems incongruous in a man who could be so callous.

Leominster (pronounced 'Lemster', as it is shown on old milestones) is the second largest town in the county, and is a phenomenon in Border history—a town of Saxon foundation which has never had a castle to defend it. Leominster was certainly not immune in the Border wars—it suffered many times at the hands of both friend and enemy.

Whatever the reason, from the thirteenth century onwards wool was indeed 'golden fleece' to Leominster, and earned the name of

'Lemster Ore'. It was praised by such diverse writers as Camden, Drayton, Izaak Walton, and Ben Johnson. Defoe thought the wool about Leominster '... the finest without exception of any in England, the South Down wool not excepted', and in more practical terms, it fetched far higher prices—nearly four times as much as the best from other parts of the country. After the Industrial Revolution, the Ryland sheep which had yielded this valuable wool were allowed almost to die out, but they are now being bred again, although the Shropshire Down, Kerry and Clun breeds are more generally kept.

Leominster faced its failing wool trade with courage and initiative, developing other trades and light industries, and in the process losing something of the past, but still cherishing many of the lovely old houses created with the wealth of its wool merchants. It is still an important market town, and a centre of the Hereford Shorthorn cattle raising industry. Some of the largest sales in the country take place there, and fantastic prices are given by dealers from North America and the Argentine.

Broad Street with its Georgian houses narrows abruptly to become the High Street, with carved timbering and projecting upper storeys, and in side streets, where there are curious names like Poplands, Bargates, The Board and Perseverance Road, houses of many periods can be found. Bridge Street has a house (No. 29) dating from 1400, and there are numerous Tudor houses in Drapers' Row.

In 1855, an Italianate town hall was built, and the old town hall and butter-market, built in 1633 by John Abel, the 'King's Carpenter', of whom more will be heard later, was taken down and sold for £95 to John Arkwright, grandson of the 'Spinning jenny Arkwright', who filled in the arcading and re-erected it on its present site as a private house. After many vicissitudes, it was bought back by the Council in 1939, for a far larger sum of money than their short-sighted predecessors had been paid. It is now known as Grange Court, and is again in use as the administrative centre of Leominster, and is surrounded by well-kept public gardens. It has been criticized with some justice as looking a little 'bogus' after various alterations and restorations, but the great richness of the carving, and its interesting architectural details, make it a splendid example of Abel's early work.

Not far from the Grange is the glory of Leominster—its great red sandstone Priory church. Nothing survives of the nunnery established by Earl Leofric and Lady Godiva, which was overtaken by a grave scandal. Sweyn, son of Earl Godwin, had tried to marry the Abbess Eadgifa, and the sequel is tersely entered in *The Anglo-Saxon Chronicle*:

A.D. 1046. This year went Earl Sweyne into Wales; and Griffin, King of the Northern men with him, and hostages were delivered to him. As he returned homeward, he ordered the Abbess of Leominster to be fetched him and he had her as long as he list, after which he let her go home.

Soon after this, the nunnery was suppressed. According to the records of Reading Abbey, it was one of three places suppressed 'because of their sins', but whether this had anything to do with the Sweyn affair is not specified. It was re-founded as a monastery, and Henry I made it a 'cell' of Reading Abbey in 1123. It remained under Reading Abbey until the Dissolution.

The church is practically all that remains. It is remarkable for its three naves, all of different periods of architecture: Norman, Early English and Decorated. The door-way of the Decorated nave has a profusion of ball-flower ornament. The most interesting possession of the Priory Church is a curious late thirteenth-century mural of the Wheel of Life. Rather unsuitably the town Ducking Stool, last used in 1809, is preserved in the church.

Leominster Out Parish, on the south and west of the town, also has some fine old houses, barns and hop-kilns. A mile south-east of Leominster a fourteenth-century farm-house, Eaton Hall, was the home of the Hakluyts, a family long settled in Herefordshire. Richard Hakluyt, of *Voyages* fame, is said to have spent his boyhood there.

The A.44 from Leominster is not only the most direct but the most enchanting route to Kington, for the way lies along the valley of the Arrow, with its villages where, in spite of the cars which replace the horses of a more leisured age, time seems to have stood still to leave them in their picture-book perfection. Each has its devotees, for each differs from the other. Pembridge clusters closely around its quaint old church, with its much-photographed, three-storied detached belfry. The lovely little sixteenth-century Market Hall has an open ground floor on timber-posts, and pyramidal roof, and there are houses dating from every period since the fourteenth century. The New Inn was built in the early 1600's, and two alms-houses date from the same century.

At Eardisland, the houses are spread out beside the shining river, with wide grassy borders alongside the road, enabling each to be appreciated to the full. The loveliest, Staick House, is known locally as the Old Vicarage. It has a great hall built about 1300 and two later wings, which form three sides of a courtyard, near the twin-arched bridge across the Arrow. Burton Court, with its fourteenth-century Hall, is open to the public in the summer. Kingsland, which lies off the main road, between the Pinsley Brook and the Lugg, has a church built by one of the Mortimers about 1300, noted for its tiny Volca chamber, which was probably a chantry chapel. Staunton-on-Arrow, also off the main road, has the delightful Court of Noke, a pedimented Queen Anne house of brick, which is a restful change from the dazzling effect of so many 'magpie' houses.

I have never visited these villages in high summer, when they are thronged with tourists, but in other seasons I have always been charmed by their exquisite neatness. I can only hope tourists respect this endearing trait.

The line of Offa's Dyke is crossed before reaching Kington, but is much broken in this neighbourhood and the south of Herefordshire, because the builders were able to leave untouched the stretches of country which were then so densely wooded they were impenetrable. Here too, the 'short' dykes are chiefly found, both east and west of the main Dyke. They differ from Offa's and Wat's Dykes in being local efforts chiefly in fertile valleys, to protect isolated farming communities. They are older than Offa's Dyke, and may date back to Penda's time.

Kington has a maze of narrow streets between the bridge over the Arrow and the church on high ground at the other end of the busy High Street, where too many of the old houses have been re-fronted, but still have the attraction of a wildly irregular skyline. Both church and town suffered from Victorian restorations and rebuildings, but the Talbot Hotel dates from 1600, and there are some good Georgian houses. The church has a Norman tower which was once detached. The chancel is Early English and the Decorated south chapel has an elaborate alabaster tomb with the effigies of Thomas Vaughan, second son of Roger Vaughan of Bredwardine, and first of the Vaughans, of Hergest Court, a Yorkist who was killed at the battle of Banbury in 1469, and his wife Ellen Gethin 'The Terrible'. She is said to have earned her nickname as a girl, when she dressed as a man to attend an archery meeting, and shot her brother's murderer through the heart.

It is generally claimed that Kington received its name from Earl Harold, in honour of Edward the Confessor, but W. H. Howse, in his booklet *Kington, Herefordshire; Memorials of an Old Town* shows that it was known as 'Chingtune' some years before Harold went there, and this spelling is shown in Domesday Book in 1086. He suggested it may have received its name from King Offa.

In comparison with other Border towns, Kington seems to have taken little part in great events. The most startling incident known in its existence did not occur until 1862, when a fire in a building where blasting powder was stored woke sleepers as far away as Eardisland with the explosion. No-one was hurt, and services of thanksgiving were held in all the churches for this miraculous deliverance.

Some of the Hutchinson relatives of Wordsworth's wife lived in Kington, and he and Dorothy Wordsworth stayed there, as well as at Hindwell. Sir Edward Elgar loved to explore the surrounding hills, and E. J. Moeran wrote some of his compositions at his parents' home at Gravel Hill, but even these associations are overshadowed by the fame of Hergest Court in its hey-day. It was a centre of Welsh culture all through the fifteenth century, but it is now only a farm-house, a fraction of its original size, a mile along the Gladestry road, with the Arrow flowing below and the steep ridge of Hergest (pro-nounced 'Hargest' with a hard 'g') towering above. It was here the *White Book of Hergest* and the *Red Book of Hergest*, with their tales of Welsh legends and folk-lore, were preserved. It is believed Lewis Glyn Cothi transcribed the *White Book of Hergest*, which was des-troyed by a fire in 1808. The *Red Book* was more fortunate, and is now in the Bodleian Library at Oxford. It was there the Welsh scholar the Rev. John Jones (Tegid) transcribed it from Old Welsh into Modern Welsh for Lady Charlotte Guest's English translation *The Mabinogion*, in which he, the Rev. Thomas Price (Carnhuanawc), Judge A. J. Johnes of Garthmyl, and other Welsh scholars gave considerable help, particularly with the voluminous notes, but for which they never received acknowledgment.

The gardens and park of Hergest Croft, a mile along the A.44 from Kington to Radnor, are open from May to June in aid of the National Gardens Scheme. I like the honesty of the stark announcement in their advertisement: 'No reasonable public transport'.

It is only 13 miles along the A.49 from Leominster to Hereford, along the Lugg Valley and over Dinmore, with turnings off it to a number of interesting villages and mansions, including Dinmore Manor, which has a fourteenth-century chapel of a Commandery of the Knights Templars, cloisters and rock garden, which are open to the public in summer.

CHAPTER NINE

Hereford and the Golden Valley

Hereford, first of the Marcher towns to be used as a base for conquering Welsh territory, is smaller than either Shrewsbury or Chester, and has closer links with the surrounding countryside. It combines to a remarkable degree the friendly atmosphere of a market town with the attributes of a cathedral city. It is a place for scholars to browse in peace among the books of the chained library—the largest in the world—or among the charters and manuscripts at the Town Hall or the Public Library, and for musicians to foregather during the triennial Three Choirs Festival.

Unlike most Border towns, it is on a level site, and is not especially striking when seen from a distance. It must be admitted that the main approaches are commonplace, but this is counterbalanced by the mature beauty of the countryside in which it is set, and its claims as a touring centre, on the central reaches of the River Wye, and midway between the Malvern hills and the Welsh mountains.

At first sight, Hereford does not appear to be an ancient city, for Georgian and Victorian frontages hide many of the sixteenth- and seventeenth-century houses, some of which have cellars dating back to the thirteenth century. The vaults at the 'Pippin' show a typical medieval cellar, now used as a public house.

The Old House, a black and white house dating from 1612, was presented to the city in 1927 by the Directors of Lloyds Bank, and is now open to the public as a Period Museum. It is beautifully furnished, chiefly with gifts from local families.

The collapse of a chimney stack in 1919 led to the discovery that the magnificent roof timbers of the Booth Hall had been hidden away behind partition floors and ceiling. It probably dates from between 1390 and 1400, for among the city's records is a licence granted by Richard II in 1392, giving permission for the erection of a 'hall where in to hold pleas'. In 1780, part of the building was converted into an inn, one of whose landlords was Tom Winter, born at Fownhope nearby in 1795. He is better remembered as Tom Spring, the pugilist who succeeded Tom Cribb in 1825 as champion of England.

In addition to the cathedral, there are two ancient churches, St Peter's, with an Early English chancel and fifteenth-century canopied choir stalls; and All Saints, mainly late thirteenth- and fourteenth-century work, with fourteenth-century canopied stalls and misericords. Its library of 300 chained books, second only to that of the cathedral in size, narrowly escaped being sold to an American for £100 at the beginning of the century.

The remains of Black Friars monastery and Preaching Cross, the Coningsby Hospital, dating from 1614, and some of the old city walls can be seen also.

Nevertheless, much has been lost, less by the misfortunes of war, than through the vandalism of Hereford's own citizens since 1800. P. Thoresby Jones, writing in 1958 in *Welsh Border Country*, says '...it is almost incredible that not so long ago some members of the Council would have sold this building (the Old House) to America to "save the rates"'.

'Conservation' is now in the air in Hereford, as elsewhere, but it is obvious vigilance is still needed. It is only a short while since one of Hereford's half-timbered houses was moved on rollers to form part of Littlewoods Store!

One thing in Hereford has remained constant: the pattern of the ancient streets inside the line of the city walls, which it is believed has continued unchanged since before the Norman Conquest. The exact date of the foundation of Hereford is in dispute. The Romans appear to have had an outpost there about A.D. 70, which they abandoned in favour of Kenchester (*Magnis*), and it was not until some time in the early seventh century that the Mercians occupied the site. The cathedral must have been founded before A.D. 676, when there is mention of the first bishop, Putta, and a Synod was held there in A.D. 680. This must have been a simple wattle building, which was rebuilt by Offa, who transformed it into 'a fair and goodly building'. This was either rebuilt or extended by Athelstan early in the eleventh century, and the present fabric was probably begun in 1080 by Bishop Robert of Lorraine, or Losinga. Work has been carried on at Hereford cathedral in almost every period since then.

Hereford possessed its own liturgy from 1215, known as 'The Hereford Use', and is one of the five Churches referred to in The Preface to the Book of Common Prayer, the others being York, Salisbury, Lincoln and Bangor.

Although the Earldom of Hereford conferred on William Fitz-osbern was forfeited even before Domesday Book was compiled, the title of 'Hereford in Wales' was used for centuries on official documents, from its close connection with the old Welsh district of Erging, known to the English as 'Archenfield', which was bounded by the Wye, Worm and Monnow, and although extending almost to the gates of Hereford, was a stronghold of Welsh customs and ideas, which it was allowed to retain under its Norman lords.

Hereford's citizens guarded their own privileges jealously, and when Edward I was establishing his new Boroughs, a 'Customary' was compiled to meet requests from other towns for advice. Copies made later preserve a vivid picture of the regulations governing Hereford's citizens at that time. Perhaps it was with memories of the ravages by the Welsh in earlier centuries that Hereford snubbed the village of Cardiff in 1284, when they applied for information, with the reply that the King's citizens of Hereford 'the principal city of all the market towns between the Severn and the sea' were bound to send their regulations freely only to towns owned by the king, and that other 'market villages' such as Cardiff must pay for the information. Hereford could hardly be expected to foresee that Cardiff would become the capital of Wales, and six times the size of Hereford!

Hereford has been more careful in preserving its ancient charters and archives than its buildings. They are kept with the magnificent City plate and insignia in the Town Hall. A set of regulations dating from the first and second years of the reign of Philip and Mary is recorded in the Historical Manuscripts Commission Report of 1892. A second set, with slight alterations, dating from 1557, was transcribed by Mr F. C. Morgan, then City Librarian, and published as a booklet in 1945, with an interesting introduction, throwing a great deal of light on life in the city during the sixteenth century. Some relate specifically to travellers.

All serving-men and others coming to the city had to leave their weapons at their inns, upon pain of forfeiture of these, and the imprisonment of the offenders, although every knight and squire of worship could have a sword borne after him. All innkeepers had to acquaint their guests with this regulation, under a 'paine of 6s. 8d.', and no person was to go abroad in the streets after 9 o'clock at 'nyghte but yef he be of good name & good Fame & have a lighte with hym'. Regulations with a more modern ring relate to 'parking' offences. All coming to the city had to put up their horses at their lodgings and not leave them in the market place.

There are so many guides to the cathedral that it must suffice here to mention its unique treasures, the Mappa Mundi, and the chained library.

The Mappa Mundi was drawn on vellum about 1300 by Richard de Bello of Haldingham, a prebendary of Hereford cathedral, and is worthy of longer study than the fleeting glance it too often receives, for it illustrates the ideas and beliefs of the Middle Ages, with their limited acquaintance with geography, their credulous belief in legends and in the existence of fabulous monsters, and their preoccupation with Rome and the East. The world is shown as a circle, with Jerusalem in the centre, Asia at the top of the map, and Europe and Africa below. The British Isles are on the outside edge, out of all proportion to the size of the rest of Europe, and the North Sea is entirely squeezed out. There are delightful little sketches of the Garden of Eden, Noah's Ark, Lot's wife, Moses on Mount Sinai and other Biblical scenes and characters, with Christ in Glory presiding over the Last Judgment, and Richard de Haldingham, the maker of the map, on horseback, with his hounds and page. There are also unicorns, vampires, and other fabled creatures and wonders, including a man using his large feet as a parasol.

The cathedral library has nearly 1,500 chained books, including 50 incunabula, among which are *The Golden Legend,* printed by Caxton in 1483, and *The Nuremburg Chronicle,* with woodcuts by Albrect Dürer, dating from 1493. The many valuable manuscripts include a ninth-century illuminated copy of the Gospels, bequeathed by Athelstan in 1055, and the thirteenth-century Hereford Breviary, with a quantity of beautifully illuminated church music, which is the only known copy of the Hereford Use with music. There are also some 30,000 documents dating from Anglo-Saxon times.

There must be something in the air of Hereford which nurtures talent, judging by the extraordinary number of distinguished people associated with this one small place. As a cathedral city, it naturally has a long list of bishops, over thirty of whom are buried in the cathedral, with resplendent tombs or brasses to commemorate them. Hereford was fortunate in having a succession of able, and often great and good bishops, but the greatest of all was St Thomas de Cantilupe, who was appointed to the see in 1275. He was a kindly gentle scholar, but could be utterly fearless in protecting his flock. Many miracles were worked at his tomb, and in his honour the Crown allowed the see to exchange its previous armorial bearings for those of the Saint, which it has borne to the present day. There is no space here to mention all the other bishops, except the one mentioned in an old ballad, who was captured by Robin Hood. It may have been Bishop William de Vere, who built the great episcopal palace, or his successor.

The Cathedral Choir had a great musical tradition long before the inauguration of the Three Choirs Festival in the early 1720's. John Dunstable, who had a European fame as a composer in the fifteenth century, had only a shadowy connection with the cathedral as a non-residentiary canon, but Dr John Bull, a master of key-board composition, was organist from 1582 to 1585. A memorial in the Bishop's Cloisters commemorates the Rev. William Felton, distinguished in his day as a composer, and for his playing of the harpsicord and piano. He was Vicar-Choral from 1714 until his death in 1769. In the nineteenth century, the Rev. Sir Frederick Ouseley, Professor of Music at Oxford, and composer of much church music, was Precentor of Hereford for 34 years, until his death in 1889. There is a memorial window to him in the south nave aisle.

Greatest of all the musicians associated with Hereford is Sir Edward Elgar, who was drawn there, like so many others, by the Three Choirs Festival. He played as a violinist in the 1878 Festival, and became a close friend of the cathedral organist, Dr G. R. Sinclair, who, with his bulldog Dan, inspired No. XI of the *Enigma Variations*. A plaque on the wall of Plas Gwyn, Hereford Park, records that Elgar lived there from 1904 to 1911; whilst there, he completed the *First Symphony*, and composed *The Kingdom*, the fourth *Pomp and Circumstance March*, and the *Wand of Youth Suites*. Even after his removal to Hampstead, he maintained a close connection with Hereford, and his last appearance as a conductor was at Hereford cathedral at the 1933 Three Choirs Festival.

The first successful performance of *The Dream of Gerontius* in this country was at the 1902 Festival. It is now played on the last night of the Festival, which is held annually in the week beginning on the first Sunday in September, in the cathedrals of Hereford, Gloucester and Worcester in rotation. It continues to draw on the services of the greatest composers, conductors and performers of the day, and is an experience not to be missed by any true lover of music.

The school which has been attached to the cathedral from since at least 1381 has produced such diverse personalities as Daniel Rowland, the great Welsh revivalist; Alfred Russell Wallace, the contemporary of Darwin; and Fred Weatherley, the lyric writer.

No-one who has the slightest knowledge of the history of the theatre will need to be told that David Garrick and 'pretty, witty' Nell Gwynn were born in Hereford, the Kembles had their home there, and Kitty Clive had associations with the town, but they may well be astonished to learn that Hereford no longer has a theatre of its own.

It would be tedious to list all the celebrities of Hereford, but I should like to mention a few 'worthies'. John Davies, the Elizabethan poet and writing master, born there about 1565, according to Fuller, was 'the greatest master of the pen that England in his age beheld for 1. *Fast writing*, so incredible was his expedition. 2. *Fair writing*, some minutes' consultation being required to decide whether his lines were written or printed. 3. *Close writing*, a mystery indeed, and too dark for my dim eyes to discover. 4. *Various writing*, Secretary, Roman, Court and Text.

John Scarlett Davies, or Davis, who made his first contribution to the Royal Academy in 1825, was the son of a shoemaker of Hereford. He showed great promise at an early age, and studied in France. His last exhibit was in 1844. David Cox lived in Hereford from 1814 to 1827, and was for a time Drawing Master at Hereford Cathedral School. He painted many local scenes, including the old Butchers Row, of which only the Old House now remains. There are good examples of the work of Davies and Cox in the Hereford Art Gallery.

The greatest of all the poor boys of Hereford who made good was Thomas Traherne, the son of a shoemaker, a poet who became Rector of Credenhill, four miles north-west of Hereford, in 1652. We shall meet him again there. One last example: Miles Smith, who died in 1624, was the son of a Hereford butcher, became a distinguished classical scholar, and won fame as an Orientalist. Wood says 'Chaldiac, Syriac, and Arabic were as familiar to him almost as his native tongue'. He was one of the translators of the Authorized Version of the Bible, for which he also wrote the Preface, and as a reward was consecrated Bishop of Gloucester in 1612.

In spite of its gradual depopulation, Herefordshire's countryside has a most reassuring and attractive look of prosperity. There are few tumbledown barns and overgrown hedges, which may be picturesque, but are a sure sign of ineptitude and poverty. Hereford, at the heart of the county, has this cultivated beauty at its doorstep, with that bright red soil of Devonian Old Red Sandstone which appears to be essential for the highest perfection of cider apple orchards.

It is not known when cider was first made in Herefordshire, but it was earning unstinted praise as early as the fifteenth century. John Gerard says in his *Herball*: 'I have seene in the pastures and hedgerows about the grounds of a worshipfull gentleman dwelling two miles from Hereford ... so many trees of all sorts, that the servants drinke for the most part no other drinke but what is made of Apples. The quantity is such, that by the report of the gentleman himselfe the Parson hath for tithe so many hogsheads of Syder. The hogs are fed with the fallings of them, which are so many, that they make choise of those Apples they do eate, who will not taste of any but of the best'. *Herefordshire Orchards, a Pattern for all England*, published early in the seventeenth century, shows the extent of apple-growing and cider-making which, as Evelyn says had 'become one continuous orchard'. *Cyder*, the best-known poem of John Philips, whose grandfather was a canon-residentiary of Hereford Cathedral, also gives such an exact account of the culture of the apple tree and the manufacture of cider that Philip Miller, the botanist, told Dr Johnson 'there were many books written on the same subject in prose, which do not contain so much truth as that poem'. The result of all this cultivation was summed up by Defoe: '...as for cyder, here it was, that several time for 20 miles together, we could get no beer or ale in their public houses, only cyder; and that so very good, so fine and so cheap, that we never found fault with the exchange; great quantities of this cyder are sent to London, even by lane carriage tho' so very remote, which is an evidence for the goodness of it beyond contradiction'.

At one time every farm had its cider press, and a few still remain, though seldom, if ever, in use since the development of the cider works started by H. P. Bulmer, son of a Rector of Credenhill, in a shed in Hereford in 1887. Bulmer's also make perry from the pear crops.

The trim hop fields, with their vines stretching along high wires, are almost all around Ledbury, where there were once extensive vineyards. Ledbury is well worth visiting for its own sake, and as the birthplace of John Masefield, and the childhood home of Elizabeth Barrett Browning, but it is rather too far east for the true Border Country.

North-west of Hereford is another group of 'show-place' black and white villages, more scattered than those in the valley of the Arrow, but which can be seen easily in a 'round trip' along the A.4110, the A.4112, and the A.438. Canon Pyon is on the A.4110, but its church, which has some good misericords, is some distance to the west, and from there a lane skirts Pyon Hill to King's Pyon, whose most attractive house is reached by a lane south to Butt House Farmstead, half

24 *Tudor rood loft, Patrishow Church*

25 *The exterior of Patrishow Church, Breconshire*

a mile west of Canon Pyon as the crow flies! The farm, with its beautiful Falconry Gatehouse, is backed by the steep slope of Nupton Hill and the oddly shaped Butthouse Knapp. Dilwyn, on the A.4112, can be reached from King's Pyon by winding lanes through a district of rich pastures and low wooded hills. Especially noteworthy at Dilwyn are the early seventeenth-century Luntley Court with its two-storeyed porch; Swanstone Court, with its mingling of fourteenth- and eighteenth-century work; and the very fine church, with its fifteenth-century nave roofs, and lofty south porch of red sandstone.

Weobley, also a little off the main road, is one of the greatest show-places of this area. It was once a borough, and still claims the dignity of a market town, although many villages are larger—and less beautiful. It is a place to be seen rather than described. It has an enormous diversity of design in its half timbering, which ranges from the fourteenth century onwards. Outstanding are the Old School House, the Red Lion, and Throne Farm, but even the wealth of half-timbering in Weobley itself should not be allowed to deter the visitor from seeking out The Ley, which lies three-quarters of a mile away across the fields, and Fenhampton, also just off the B.4230. The Ley was built by James Bridges in 1589 and is by general consent the loveliest, as it is one of the largest timber framed houses in the county, with its founder's coat of arms above the porch. The road to the long, two-storeyed Fenhampton passes the entrance gates to Garnstone, which was bought by Col. Birch, the Parliamentarian commander, who quarrelled with Cromwell and played a leading part in the restoration of Charles II, and managed to acquire a great deal of property and wealth in the process. There is a huge wall monument to his memory in Weobley church. Two effigies in the church commemorate Sir Walter Devereux, who married Agnes Crophill, heiress of Weobley Castle, who died in 1402, and his widow and her second husband Sir John Marbury 'doorkeeper to Henry the Fifth'.

Charles I had supper at an inn in Weobley on 5 September 1645. Was the luckless king cheered by a draught or two of the famous Weobley ale, which was so highly praised by Camden in his *Britannia*?

Returning to the A.4112, the retiring little village of Sarnesfield must surely be visited, if only to pay tribute to John Abel, who contributed so much to the beauty of the Herefordshire towns and villages. The church is partly Norman and is notable for the dove-cote in its tower, which has nesting holds for 100 doves. Abel's plain altar tomb is in the churchyard, near the timbered porch. Curiously enough, although Abel raised the building of black and white houses to its greatest perfection, and influenced all later timber-framed houses, he did not obtain his title of The King's Carpenter for his architectural triumphs, but as a reward for making mills to grind corn when Hereford was besieged by the Scots in 1645. After he was 90 years of age, the hale old man prepared his own tombstone, engraving it with his own effigy, kneeling with his two wives, and the emblems of his occupation, with a long epitaph he had composed. He died in 1674, at the age of 97.

Kinnersley, south-west along the A.4112, is a hamlet on high ground, with a sixteenth-century manor-house and a twelfth-century church largely rebuilt in the following centuries, which has wood-work of many periods, and a florid Carolean monument to the Smallman family who lived at the manor-house. North of Kinnersley is Almeley (Elm Meadow), which was once a place of importance, owned by the powerful Walter de Beauchamp in the time of King John. Only the mound and some earthworks remain of this castle, and an earlier castle on a neighbouring mound has vanished com-pletely. There is a medieval manor-house and a seventeenth-century Meeting House. The church tower dates from 1200, the chancel and vestry from a century later, and the sixteenth-century nave roof is painted with Tudor roses. A short distance from the village is Nieu-port (or Newport) House, which is even more interesting to me, personally, because in collecting material for a biography of Ben-jamin Hall (afterwards Lord Llanover) the man after whom 'Big Ben' was named, I discovered it was here he spent the first year and a half of his married life, and that his eldest child was born. After the 1939-45 war it became a Latvian Convalescent Home. His home for the rest of his life was at Llanover, near Abergavenny, in the valley of the Usk.

Back again on the A.4112, it is only a couple of miles to its junc-tion with the A.4111, and just north of this is Eardisley, which consists almost entirely of one long street, chiefly of black and white houses, one of which is an interesting fourteenth-century cruck house. The medieval church has an eighteenth-century tower, and a wonderfully carved Norman tub font. The fighting warriors resemble those at Kilpeck, particularly in the treatment of their hair, but the less learned in such matters will delight in the carving on the other side—the look of disappointment on the lion's face as he is deprived of his victim is irresistibly comic. It is an outstanding example of the work of the Herefordshire School of sculpture.

Near the church is the mound which is all that remains of the important castle of Eardisley, a stronghold of Roger Lacy, and later owned by the Bohuns and the Baskervilles. It was here Peter of Aigueblanche (Peter Aquablanca) Bishop of Hereford, who was seized by the barons in his own cathedral at the start of the Baron's War, was 'closely confined' for three months, having 'made himself odious to the realm by his intolerable exactions' on behalf of Henry III. He was one of the most able, if one of the least loved, of the Bishops of Hereford, and was the king's trusted adviser—as well he might be, for he was not above extortion and chicanery to help fill his royal master's coffers, not forgetting his own. Henry gave him the bishopric of Hereford in 1240, and he held it until his death, although frequently abroad for long periods on the king's business. He packed the chapter with his kinsfolk, which did not increase his popularity, but he was extremely liberal to the cathedral, and strenuous in defence of its liberties against 'the citizens of Hereford and other rebels'. He built himself a sumptuous tomb in Hereford cathedral, which can be seen there still.

There was a time when Eardisley not only had its own station, on the Hereford, Hay and Brecon line, but was a junction for the G.W.R. line from Eardisley to Kington and New Radnor, which became the centre of one of those bitter railway disputes of the late nineteenth century. The Hereford to Brecon line had been started as a private enterprise by that energetic promoter and builder of railways, Thomas Savin, but was acquired in 1874 by the Midland Railway, with the idea of linking their main line routes with Swansea. The move was successfully countered by the G.W.R., who eventually took over the line when railways were nationalized.

Today, neither this nor any of the other branch lines and narrow-gauge railways which made such an extraordinary network over the district, are in existence. I travelled on all those which survived the 1914-18 war, and lament their passing, as everyone must do who knew them. Most of them passed through finer scenery than the road services which superseded them, and many had involved almost incredible feats of engineering. I am glad I knew them, and delighted that at least a few of them are being revived by railway enthusiasts.

The most direct road back to Hereford is along the north bank of the ever-winding Wye, which is frequently too far from the road to be discerned. A variation can be made by turning off at Bridge Sollers to Kenchester, in level fields below wooded Credenhill. It is interesting only as the site of the Roman town of *Magnis*, on the road from *Deva* to *Isca*, of which all that remains is a small portion of a wall, and a font made from a Roman column in the little Norman church. All other relics are in the museum in Hereford.

Credenhill, rising 700 feet, is crowned with an Iron Age camp. The village with its attractive church is on the southern slopes. A tablet in the church, belatedly set up in 1908, commemorates the Rev. Thomas Traherne, who was Rector of Credenhill from 1657 to 1667, with a quotation from his own *Centuries of Meditation* which sums up his life and work: 'He had a deep and perfect sense of all the glories and pleasures that in God's works are hid'.

Traherne was of true Border descent for at least six centuries, and in spite of his own humble birth, his family was related to the ancient chieftains of Brecheiniog and Powys. He evolved as one of the metaphysical poets of the seventeenth century, who had the same combination of Welsh and English ancestry which seems to have been an essential ingredient of their development. Less fortunate than his contemporaries, his work had to wait until this century to gain recognition. His manuscripts, after many vissicitudes, were rescued from a book barrow in London in 1895, and were at first attributed to Henry Vaughan. His *Poetical Works* were first published in 1906, and his prose works, *Centuries of Meditation*, in 1908. No book about the Welsh Border makes any mention of him before H. J. Massingham's deeply appreciative tribute in *The*

Southern Marshes, which must have sent many to his works for the first time, although he is still far too little known and valued. He led a simple and devout life, and his earlier poems, which contain his best poetic work, and his even more attractive prose, which has a limpid, singing quality all its own, show a child-like harmony with and delight in the natural world.

South and west of Hereford are the old Welsh districts of Erging (Archenfield), which lie roughly in the triangle between the Wye, the Monnow and the modern A.465, and Ewyas, between the River Ewyas and the Dore, where there are long, narrow mountain glens threaded by rivers running south to join the Monnow. Both districts came early under Saxon rule, and subsequently under Norman rule, but were permitted to retain their old Welsh laws and customs until at least the end of the twelfth century. Welsh saints were honoured there, and St David had an important church at Much Dewchurch. St Dyfrig (*Dubricius*) was, by tradition, born at Madley. The people of Archenfield and Ewyas became fiercely loyal to the Norman lords, even against their own countrymen, and are today more English than Welsh, yet there are still lingering traces of their Welsh origin in their personal names, place-names and their legends, and in the lilting inflection of their voices. Perhaps it is not surprising that two of the most successful of the smaller Music Festivals of recent years are to be found there.

The way to the Golden Valley runs for some miles through a peaceful countryside with few particularly outstanding features, and gives little hint of the jewel hidden away down a lane from St Devereux—Kilpeck, the tiny, attractive village with the most wonderful little church in the county—some say, in all England. Not even the best photographs can convey fully the magnificence of the carving on the arches inside and outside the church—carved so deeply into the red sandstone that even the ravages of over eight centuries of weathering have not effaced their detail and interest.

Architecturally, Kilpeck remains unaltered since it was built about 1136, and although the rood-screen has vanished, for once this is not to be regretted, for it is the unrestricted view of the apsidal sanctuary which makes the little church so impressive.

The riot of carving shows a combination of piety, precept,

mockery, and sheer sense of fun, and is the best surviving example of the Herefordshire School of sculpture, about whose origins there are numerous theories. Kilpeck, conscious of its responsibilities, has produced an attractive guide which incorporates extracts from an earlier booklet by Mr F. C. Morgan, and from the Royal Commission on the *Historical Monuments of Herefordshire.*

The plain, whitewashed walls of Kilpeck throw the carved red sandstone arches and bosses into sharp relief, and add to the feeling of simplicity and devotion the church engenders. It is a place to linger in, but there is another treasure nearby, although of a different kind, in Abbey Dore, in the tranquil Golden Valley. The valley lies between the Black Mountains rising to 2,300 feet, and gentle hills which are barely above 300 feet in height, and is watered by the River Dore, which rises in the hills above Dorstone, and joins the Monnow near Pontrilas.

The early history of the region was as stormy as any other on the Border. Herefordshire has the doubtful honour of having the earliest castle in the country, for the word 'castle' first occurs in English records in 1048, when the *Anglo-Saxon Chronicle* used it to describe the innovation introduced by Norman protégés of Edward the Confessor, one of whom had built a 'castle' in Herefordshire, and it is probable that the 'Pentecost' castle mentioned in the Chronicle in 1052 was at Ewyas, although the reference may be to Richard's castle.

Only a lofty conical mound and some earthworks remain, without a trace of masonry, beside the road which leads through Dulas, which has a church noted for its Jacobean woodwork, to Longtown, with the remains of the cylindrical keep of the Lacy's castle, set where the Ochon, and the Escley Brook emerge from their valleys to meet and mingle with the Monnow River.

Ewyas Harold took its second name from a Norman lord identified by different writers about the Border as a great-grand-nephew of Edward the Confessor; a grandson or great-nephew of the Conqueror; and a grandson or great nephew of William Fitzosbern, of which the last-named seems to be the most likely.

There is a delightful view from the castle mound across the Dulas Brook to the much-restored Early English church, which has the effigy of a woman clasping a heart, and a cynical epitaph in the churchyard:

> *Reader pass on, nor waste your time*
> *On bad biography, and much worse rhyme,*
> *For what I am this cumbrous clay immures,*
> *And what I was is no concern of yours,*

after reading which, there is nothing to do but hurry on to Abbey Dore (Dŵr), a magnificent survival standing somewhat forlornly among fields, with one of its lychgates reached through a farmyard. In spite of this rather unpromising start, it is a beautiful and well-cared-for church, enshrining all that is left of the Cistercian abbey, whose monks were so ruthlessly castigated by Giraldus Cambrensis, in his usual racy style, in his *Spectrum Ecclesiae.*

At the Dissolution, the abbey was granted to John Scudamore of Holme Lacy, whose descendant, John, first Viscount Scudamore, so well-deserved his title of 'The Good Lord Scudamore'. He disliked possessing Church property, and commissioned John Abel to restore Abbey Dore, the condition of which was then so bad that cattle used it for shelter. The roof was rebuilt of Herefordshire oak, 204 tons being used, at a cost of 5s. a ton. A service of consecration took place in 1634, and since then the church has been one of the very few Cistercian churches in England in regular use for worship.

Here again, Mr F. C. Morgan has provided an excellent account. of the church and its treasures. To me, its most striking feature is the spacious, uncluttered west end, with the rather heavy, but undeniably impressive wooden screen carved by John Abel blocking the view of the nave and chancel, in striking contrast with the lovely simplicity of the Early English architecture at the eastern end of the presbytery.

Unlike the Festival at Madley, a few miles north in the Wye Valley, which is organized entirely by local people, the Abbey Dore Festival was founded by two friends working in London, who agreed with Sir John Betjeman that 'no county has a church so wonderful as Abbey Dore'. Artists of international reputation are engaged, and funds are raised for preserving the structure of the Abbey.

Just beyond Abbey Dore, a turning off the main road (B.4347) leads to Bacton, óne of the most attractive villages in the valley, with a church notable for an altar frontal depicting a boat with two passengers, and formalized birds, beasts, flowers and insects, embroidered in colours on white silk. It is said to be the work of Blanche Parry, whose effigy shows her kneeling before her mistress, Elizabeth I, with an epitaph recording 'Wyith maeden Quene, a maed dyd ende my lyffe'.

Blanche Parry, who was born at Bacton about 1508, was related to the Vaughans of Bredwardine and Tretower, the Herberts, the Stradlings of St Donats, and other Welsh families, and was a kinswoman of the great Cecil, Lord Burghley, who drew up her will, and was her chief executor. She became 'Gentlewoman' to Elizabeth when she was a princess only three years old, and remained in the queen's confidence and service until her death in 1590. The extent of her influence over the queen has been a constant source of speculation for centuries, and many stories are told about her, but her career has been elucidated fully by C. A. Bradford in *Blanche Parry, Queen Elizabeth's Gentlewoman*. Although she had prepared the tomb at Bacton for herself, she is buried in Westminster Abbey.

Near the meeting of the B.4347 and B.4348 is Vowchurch, another of the villages in the Golden Valley which are worth turning off the main road to see. It has a sixteenth-century Old Vicarage, and a church with a profusion of carved woodwork. On a wooded hill to the east is Monnington Court, near the oval motte which is probably the site of the older mansion of the Scudamores, one of whom married Owain Glyn Dŵr's daughter, Alice. Of the many traditions about his death and burial, the most likely is that he sought refuge with his daughter and son-in-law in their secluded manor of Monnington Straddel—not to be confused with Monnington-on-Wye, as is so frequently done, and even by that usually most reliable of topographers, A. G. Bradley.

The church tower and truncated 'spire' of Peterchurch, which have an unfortunate resemblance to a factory chimney, are visible for some distance before the long village street is reached, and give no indication of the remarkable interior of the largely untouched Norman church.

The last village in the Golden Valley before reaching Hay-on-Wye is Dorstone, with the great cromlech known as Arthur's Stone on the ridge above.

CHAPTER TEN

The Wye Valley

Ever since the beauties of natural scenery were 'discovered' in the eighteenth century, travellers have enthused over the charms of the Wye Valley. The wonder is that it has been so little spoiled. A few concessions have been made to 'progress'—a camping and caravan site or two in the most popular areas; a few petrol pumps and car parks—but there are many miles in which such things can be forgotten. There are seldom, if ever, any long traffic jams, and if the road on the right bank—usually the most frequented—is too busy, there is an equally lovely road on the left bank for almost the whole of the way.

The Wye (Afon Gwy) enters Radnorshire a mile or two below Llangurig, and between Rhayader (Rhaeadr Gwy) and Rhydspence the greater part of its winding course forms the boundary between Radnorshire and Breconshire.

A many-arched bridge over the Wye links Builth Wells (Llanfair-ym-Muallt) with Llanelwedd, on the Radnorshire bank, which is the permanent site of the Royal Welsh Agricultural Show, held there in July each year. Builth is a centre for districts which were always under Welsh rule until the Edwardian conquest. On the south, the moorland heights of Mynydd Eppynt make a fine background to the Breconshire bank of the Wye, and its wide, open spaces are an invitation to strong walkers. Unfortunately, the western half is covered with extensive firing ranges, and it is necessary to keep east of the B.4519 to make sure of surviving.

At Aberedw the Wye flows for over a mile below the Aberedw Rocks, a fantastic cliff rising precipitously for 700 feet, of limestone slabs so regular they appear to be dry-walled masonry, with bushes and trees clinging to every ledge. In the tree-shaded valley down which the little Edw tumbles to join the Wye is the village and church of Aberedw, high above the river. The Early English church has a plain tower, a spacious timbered porch, a hammerbeam nave roof, and a fifteenth-century screen. Farther up the flashing stream a packhorse bridge leads up the glen to Court Farm, an ancient home of the Baskerville family.

At Erwood, a steep road with hairpin bends, on the Radnorshire side of the river, leads up to the isolated fourteenth-century church of Llandeilo Graban, where there are splendid views from the churchyard. The road continues over the hills past the lonely, reedy little Llan Bwch-llyn, to the remote parish of Llanbedr-Painscastle (Llanbedr Castellpaen), with its thirteenth-century church at Llanbedr, and the village of Painscastle a mile away. Only the motte remains of the castle, which was also known as 'Maud's Castle' after its successful defence in 1130 by Maud de St Valery, wife of the unspeakable William de Braose. The castle is one of those claimed to be the original of the 'Garde Doloureuse' of Scott's novel, *The Betrothed*, largely on the strength of the punning translation of the name!

There are several roads from Painscastle to Glasbury, Llowes and Clyro. None of them are very direct, and they have steep gradients.

Boughrood (pronounced Bockrood) and Llyswen are linked by a bridge across the river, below which the Wye rushes tumultuously among its rocks to Glasbury, the road to which passes the Three Cocks, once an important stage on the old-coach road, and still a famous inn. It retains the gates to the stairs and doors worked by bobbin latches, and other signs of its age which make it a delightful place in which to stay. The Three Cocks were the arms of the Williams family of nearby Gwernyfed.

There are good roads on either side of the river from Glasbury (Y Clas-ar-Wy), although as it wanders ever more erratically, it becomes increasingly difficult to see it until the valley narrows again in Monmouthshire. Most people will keep to the Radnorshire bank, at least as far as Hay, seeing the rampant Victorian Gothic of Maesllwch Castle, but too frequently missing the more retiring Maesyronen Chapel, a mile from the main road, on a steep hill above the Wye. It is one of the earliest Nonconformist chapels in Wales;

a plain little building, but utterly satisfying in the perfection of its proportions. It is still fitted with its seventeenth-century furniture.

The Llowes wheel-cross formerly in the churchyard is now in the church. It is said to date from the sixth century, but V. E. Nash-Williams describes it in his *Early Christian Monuments of Wales* as a 'Latin wheel-cross of Celtic (Irish) type, with a Latin cross on the back, dating from the eleventh century'. It has long been known as 'Moll Walbee's stone'. It is said that 'Moll', the Maud de St Valery who defended Painscastle, dropped it into her shoe as she was carrying an apronful of stones to rebuild Hay Castle in a single night. Finding the stone troublesome, she picked it out of her shoe and threw it to Llowes!

All this part of the Wye is in the district the Rev. Francis Kilvert knew so well, and at his beloved Clyro there is a plaque on Ashbrook House, recording it was his home from 1865 to 1872. It is pleasant to find how little the village has been changed outwardly by the number of visitors who have been drawn there after reading his *Diary*.

Mr William Plomer did a service not only to literature, but to the social history of the late Victorian era, when he rescued and published the *Diary*. Kilvert had a keenly observant eye, and the power to convey his pleasure in the lovely scenery around Clyro. He was also the best kind of parish priest, with a deep concern for the unfortunate among his flock. As we accompany him on his visits to humble cottages or great mansions, and on his long walks, we can share with him a way of life which has vanished for ever, and have a far more intimate knowledge of the period than can ever be gained from even the best sociological studies.

Kilvert has by no means been forgotten here, and the Kilvert Society, founded in Hereford in 1948, has done much to promote a wider interest in the man and his *Diary*.

It is only a mile from Clyro to Hay-on-Wye (Y Gelli), set on a hill in Breconshire, where Wales and England meet at the Dulas Brook, and Radnorshire is just over the Wye. As the pivot of two mountain regions, and of the valleys of the Wye and Dore, it is as advantageously placed for tourists as it once was for hostile invaders. It is traditionally divided into Welsh Hay and English Hay (an

Anglicized form of La Haie—an enclosure), and is still sometimes called The Haye.

Between the town and the rebuilt church is the large motte of the original Norman castle built by William de Braose or, if legend can be believed, by his wife, Maud de St Valery, and in the centre of the town is what remains of a later castle and the Jacobean mansion with which its ruins were incorporated. Traces of the old town walls can be seen along the Hereford road. The rest of the town, without having any very outstanding building, is a pleasant jumble of old and new, in streets which are especially lively on market days. Footpaths over the Black Mountains, for experienced walkers, lead to the Ochon, Escley and Monnow Valleys and to the Valley of the Honddu, through wonderful mountain scenery, but there are no direct roads for cars.

Lower down the valley of the Wye there are rival claims to interest on either side the river. The Rhydspence Inn on the left bank is right on the boundary between Wales and England, its Tudor black and white heralding the beginning of the black and white towns and villages of Herefordshire. Clifford, on the opposite bank, has the ruins of a castle in which it is said Rosamund Clifford ('Rosa Mundi') was born, but they are of later date, and the Cliffords owned many castles. There is no certainty even of the date of her birth, much less of the place. Henry II himself proclaimed his love for her, but the innumerable legends which have gathered round the memory of 'Fair Rosamund' appear to have little foundation in fact. The church, half a mile away, has one of the 96 wooden effigies which survive in Great Britain. It may represent a Rector of Clifford between 1270 and 1280, and is a beautiful piece of carving, with graceful folds in the chasuble, and reposeful features.

There is a toll bridge across the river just before reaching Whitney, and again a choice of routes to Hereford. Along the left bank the hills recede so far that the road is as dull as it is possible for any road to be in the Wye Valley, in spite of occasional low hills and a string of black and white villages, and a stretch of Offa's Dyke between Byford and Bridge Sollers. Monnington-on-Wye is in the water meadows between the A.438 and the river. It may be as well to repeat that in spite of the guide books, this Monnington must yield to Monnington Straddel in the Golden Valley as the last refuge of Owain Glyn Dŵr. The court and church were rebuilt after the Restoration of Charles II. The church has all its furnishings delightfully in keeping—oak benches like settles, and twisted barley sugar shafts wherever they could be used, with a magnificent painted coat of arms making a welcome splash of colour on the nave wall.

On the southern bank of the Wye the B.4352 passes through or near villages which are not only beautiful in themselves, but each of which has some special attraction.

The road runs between the Wye and the Merbach Hill and its outlier the Knapp, at the western end of Bredwardine, loveliest of the villages on the Herefordshire reach of the Wye. It has an attractive brick bridge across the river, neighboured by the vicarage where Kilvert lived for the last two years of his life, and the church he showed his father with so much pride. It has queer Norman carvings over the south door and the 'devil's door', and two effigies, one of an unidentified knight, and the other almost certainly the Sir Richard Vaughan who died at Agincourt. Kilvert is buried in the churchyard.

Beyond Bredwardine the road runs between Moccas Deer Park, with almost incredibly venerable trees, and the Home Park of Moccas Court, a severely Classical brick house designed by Robert Adam, with a richly decorated interior, in grounds laid out by Capability Brown. A turning on the left in the hamlet of Moccas leads to the early Norman church, which is largely built of tufa (petrified peat), and is a simpler and partly restored version of Kilpeck, with fourteenth-century stained glass in the windows, showing the arms of the de Fresne family, on a banner carried by two yellow-clad figures. The effigy in the chancel is believed to be a de Fresne who died about 1330.

Tyberton with its brick and timber-framed houses, has a brick church designed in 1720 by John Wood, the architect who designed the famous Crescent at Bath. The church has retained most of its contemporary furnishing, including box pews and an elaborately carved reredos. It incorporates the door of an earlier church on the site. Tyberton Court was demolished recently, but its ornamental grounds give the church an unusually attractive setting, although doubtless, in the course of time, they will revert to the wild.

Beyond Tyberton the road strikes away from the long wooded ridge of hills which hides the Golden Valley, to Madley, with its unusually large parish church. The fabric was begun about 1120 and finished in 1320, and was given elaborately carved woodwork in the Jacobean period. There are some ornate monuments, and a fine fourteenth-century churchyard cross. The annual Music Festival inaugurated in 1966, and usually held in June, is organized by the local people, who provide a feast of music of the highest standard.

A little to the north-east of Madley is the attractive village of Eaton Bishop, which has a church exceptional in the southern Marches for a glorious east window filled with fourteenth-century stained glass. There are other fragments of the period in the south and north windows of the chancel, and the view from the churchyard of the Black Mountains on the south-west and the Malvern Hills on the east, is alone worth the detour on a clear day.

It is only six and a half miles from Madley to Hereford, where the river begins to flow in a southerly direction, with many a bend, the first below Dinedor Hill, crowned by an Iron Age camp, and skirted by the B.4399, which keeps as close to the river as its bends will permit, as far as Fownhope. Holme Lacy, midway between Dinedor and Fownhope, is dominated by the largest country house in Herefordshire, the ancient home of the Scudamores, rebuilt in the 1670's and adorned with some of the finest plaster ceilings and carved wooden overmantels in England, some of which are now in the Metropolitan Museum in New York. The house is now a home for the aged and mentally sick. It is not easily seen from the road, but a short walk up the drive brings it into view.

The little fourteenth-century church, a mile away near the river, has many monuments to the Scudamores, including one who was a friend of Thomas Bodley, and a benefactor of his library, and another who was the 'Sir Scudamore, pattern of chivalry' in the fourth book of Spenser's *Faerie Queene*, but of all the illustrious family who lie there, none was so admirable as John Scudamore, first Viscount Scudamore, a renowned scholar and ambassador to France but, far more, a pattern of the best type of country landowner. Kindly, generous to a fault, and ever promoting the welfare of others, it was he who improved the local breeds of horses, introduced the Red

Streak Pippin, one of the best cider apples of Herefordshire, grafted and planted orchards, and almost certainly founded the Hereford breed of cattle, and in all ways contributed to the prosperity of his native county.

It is possible to reach Ross-on-Wye from Holme Lacy, by a round-about route, and there is an intricate network of lanes leading to Much Marcle and other innumerable delightful villages and good view points, but it is a district to roam at random, in the certainty of finding something rewarding, but which it is impossible to deal with adequately here.

The direct road (A.49) is less beautiful, and never touches the river at all until it crosses Wilton Bridge into Ross, but also has beguiling by-ways. Soon after leaving Hereford, Aconbury Hill can be seen. Three hundred feet higher than its neighbour Dinedor, crowned by a prehistoric camp which has been occupied in various periods, even including the Civil War, the summit commands an all-embracing view of Merbach Hill, Hay Bluff, the Sugar Loaf and the Skirrid, and even the Radnorshire hills, in good atmospheric conditions.

Aconbury church is all that is now left of an Augustinian Priory for nuns founded in the reign of King John. The excellent little guide to the church gives some details of the Prioresses, who seem to have been truly good and saintly women, and says it was Dame Isabella Gardiner, Prioress from 1489 to 1534, who brought the Dwarf Elder to Aconbury, where it still grows in abundance. There are several ancient tombs in the church, and the Royal Arms of Queen Victoria hang in the nave—a rare example in so late a reign. Aconbury is one of the few churches in England said to be haunted. The story is recorded in an old book that the ghost is a monk, dressed in habit and cowl; a surprising ghost in such a well-conducted nunnery!

The church narrowly escaped serious damage in the 1939-45 war, when a bomb fell within 200 yards of it.

Half-way is the village of Much Birch, with a delightful timbered inn and a restored churchyard cross, and a mile from Ross is Wilton Bridge, largely rebuilt to cope with modern traffic. The red sandstone castle which was built to defend the ford in Stephen's reign, before the bridge was thought of, was burnt by Sir Henry Lingen

26   *The River Usk at Crickhowell*

27 *Llanover Church and the River Usk*

28 *The Sugar Loaf, near Abergavenny, from Hatteral Hill, Black Mountains*

and Barnabas Scudamore, both ardent royalists, to 'cure Sir Facing Bothe-Wayes (Sir John Bridges) who could not decide his allegiance', with the not unnatural result he became a staunch Parliamentarian. The estate was acquired by Thomas Guy, a London 'worthy' whose connections with Herefordshire were tenuous, but who ranks with Lord Scudamore and the 'Man of Ross' for goodness of heart and care for the poor. Under his will of 1724 it came into the possession of the London hospital he had founded, and which still bears his name.

Ross-on-Wye on its low hill above the river, has long been one of those perfect English towns which are unsurpassable in their friendly atmosphere and old-world charm, but how much longer it will remain so is problematical, now that the 'Ross Spur' motorway (M.50) links it with the M.5. The handsome red sandstone Market Hall in the steep, narrow main street, was built in 1670 and incorporates parts of the previous Booth Hall. It stands on stone pillars designed by John Abel, and has a bust of Charles II in the east gable end.

Opposite the Market House is the 'Man of Ross' House. John Kyrle was another of those Englishmen who are truly to be numbered as 'worthies' for their kindliness, generosity and zeal in promoting the interests of their neighbourhood, and in their benefactions to those poorer than themselves.

Although it is over 250 years since the 'Man of Ross' died, the town he loved still benefits by his good deeds. He died in 1714, and is buried in the parish church. His simple retiring nature was such that he might have died unremembered had not Pope, who frequently stayed at Holme Lacy, extolled his virtues in his *Moral Essays*. The Kyrle Society, founded in 1877, also did much to perpetuate his memory, by giving popular concerts and promoting the conversion of waste plots of ground into gardens, to brighten the lives of the working classes in many of England's industrial cities.

Every guide book to Ross or the Wye Valley (and there are many!) rightly sings the praises of the 'Man of Ross'. They also point out that Dickens met his friend and biographer, John Forster, in the Royal Hotel in September 1867, and decided upon his American Reading Tour of 1867-8. Sherlockians do not need to be told that

Ross and its neighbourhood are the setting for *The Boscombe Valley Mystery*, and try to identify the inn at which Sherlock Holmes and Dr Watson stayed, and the possible location of Hatherley Farm and Boscombe Pool.

Another, almost forgotten, literary association is with Captain Mayne Reid, whose boys' adventure stories were founded on the actual adventures of the Irish-born author, who was even more handsome, dashing and enterprising than the heroes of his books. Dumas said of Mayne Reid's first book, *The Rifle Rangers*, that he could not close it until he had read the last word. After his incredible adventures in the American backwoods, and in every state of the Union, during which he organized a hunting expedition for the famous naturalist Audubon, Mayne Reid fought in the Mexican War, performing feats of heroism for which he received a pension from the American Government. He returned to England finally in 1870 and spent the last years of his life at Frogmore, Weston-under-Penyard, two miles from Ross, writing *Gwen Wynn, A Romance of the Wye*, breeding Welsh mountain sheep, and growing potatoes from Mexican seed. He contributed valuable articles to the *Live Stock Journal*, and as a final curious contrast to his previous adventurous life, wrote a treatise on the rules of croquet. He died in 1883 at the age of 65, and was buried in Kensal Green cemetery.

Below Ross, the Wye wanders so erratically about the country that it must be a purely personal choice whether to take the A.40 through Whitchurch to Monmouth, or the more roundabout route (B.4228) through Walford and English Bicknor, and Staunton on the A.4136.

The finest way of all is, of course, by rowing boat, although the distance is more than double that by road, and should only be attempted by experienced oarsmen, after consultation with local boatmen about the weirs and other hazards to be encountered. Below Tintern, it is essential to make the trip at high water.

This part of the Wye, down to the estuary at Chepstow, is the most frequented, and the best served by guide books. Among the many places of interest which can be seen by boat, and can also be reached by road, the first is Goodrich Castle, the only castle in Herefordshire which has remained fairly perfect, with some fine towers and walls.

During the Civil Wars of 1642-46, the garrison held out under Sir Henry Lingen until all the other Herefordshire castles had fallen, and did not yield until the Parliamentarians under Col. Birch used 'Roaring Meg' to bombard it. 'Roaring Meg' is preserved on the Castle Green at Hereford, and some of the cannon balls, weighing 200 lbs., can be seen at Goodrich.

Just north-west of Kerne Bridge are the remains of the fourteenth-century Flanesford Priory, parts of which have been built into a barn of the farm occupying the site.

About half a mile south of Goodrich Castle was the extravagantly castellated Goodrich Court, built in 1827 by Sir Samuel Rush Meyrick, after he had failed in his attempt to buy Goodrich Castle. He had rooms designed especially to accommodate his magnificent collection of armour. He was consulted by the authorities of the Tower of London as to the arrangement of the national collection of arms and armour, and at the request of George IV, arranged the collection of armour at Windsor Castle. He wrote many books on antiquarian subjects, edited Lewis Dwnn's *Heraldic Visitations of Wales and Part of the Marches* for the Welsh Manuscript Society, and a three-volume book on armour which is still a standard work.

His collection was dispersed some years after his death, and Goodrich Court, which Wordsworth, who loved the Wye Valley, had called 'an impertinence', was dismantled a few years ago and shipped to the United States of America, where it was re-erected. *Ye Olde Hostelrie* in Goodrich village, which dates from 1830, gives some slight idea of what Goodrich Court looked like.

Below Kerne Bridge the river forms the boundary between Herefordshire on the right bank and Gloucestershire on the left bank, and the scenery grows ever more beautiful.

Welsh Bicknor, which was formerly a detached part of Monmouthshire and is now, in spite of its name, in Herefordshire, is on a bend of the river, above which is Courtfield, where Henry V is said to have been brought up in the care of the Countess of Salisbury, but the present house was built long after his time. Courtfield was a seat of a branch of the Vaughans who remained Roman Catholics in spite of much persecution. In the nineteenth century Henry and Roger Vaughan, the two eldest sons of Col. John Vaughan and his wife, Louisa (daughter of John Rolls of the Hendre and aunt of the first Baron Llangattock) became respectively Cardinal Archbishop of Westminster Cathedral, and Roman Catholic Archbishop of Sidney, Australia. Courtfield is now a home of retirement for Roman Catholic priests.

In a wooded gorge beneath the steep Coldwell Rocks, the river begins the extraordinary horseshoe bend overlooked by Symonds Yat Rock, the most famous viewpoint on the Wye. The river takes four miles to reach a point which is only 500 yards away over land, and then flows south and west around the Great and Little Doward, two wooded hills separated by a narrow valley. On the riverside face of Little Doward are the 'Seven Sisters', a series of gaunt rocks contrasting with their densely wooded surroundings, and overlooking Martin's Pool, where the brilliant plumage of darting kingfishers gleams above the water. All this, and more, can be seen in the incomparable view from Symonds Yat, which takes its name from Robert Symonds, a High Sheriff of Herefordshire, who owned extensive property in the neighbourhood in the seventeenth century, and 'Yat', a word used in the Forest of Dean to mean a gate or pass.

The Wye finally leaves Herefordshire at its confluence with the Monnow (Afon Mynwy), four miles short of Monmouth (Trefynwy), still the county town of Monmouthshire (Sir Fynwy), although it has been so greatly outstripped in size by other places in the county, and above all, by Newport, which is now the administrative centre.

The most attractive approach to Monmouth is on the south-west, by the bridge across the Monnow, and on a first visit it is worth while to circle the town and enter by the Monnow Gate. Built in 1262, it is the only example of a fortified road bridge surviving in the British Isles, and is so outstandingly picturesque that it figures on practically every advertisement and booklet advertising the town.

Everyone who is familiar with Shakespeare's *Henry v* knows that the victor of Agincourt was born in the town, but it was a monk in the Priory, Geoffrey of Monmouth, who had a more far-reaching and lasting effect with his *Historium Britonum* and its glorification of King Arthur. The undistinguished fragments of the castle in which

Henry V was born stand forlornly beside a seventeenth-century house, and the Priory has vanished. The window pointed out as 'Geoffrey's' dates from at least two centuries later than his time.

Monmouth is a typically lively, bustling little Border town, and still has some pleasant old houses and inns, including one in which Admiral Lord Nelson stayed with Lady Hamilton in 1802, when he was given the Freedom of the Borough. The most unexpected attraction in Monmouth is its Nelson Museum, with the unrivalled collection of relics left to the town under the will of Lady Llangattock.

Lady Llangattock's son, the Hon. Charles Stewart Rolls, a pioneer of aviation and motoring, is commemorated by a striking statue by my old friend, the late Sir William Goscombe John, in front of the eighteenth-century Shire Hall. Rolls formed the C. S. Rolls firm which became Rolls-Royce Ltd in 1904, and in 1910 he was the first man to fly across the Channel from England to France and back without landing. A singularly ungainly and unattractive statue of Henry V 'adorns' the front of the Shire Hall itself.

Monmouth commands the way from the Midland Plains into the central passes of Wales and has always been recognized for its strategic value. The Romans had a fort nearby at *Blestium*, which was an important link in their defence of the Roman roads of Wales.

It was to defend Monmouth that the 'Three Castles', also sometimes called 'The Trilateral' were built—Skenfrith and Grosmont on the Upper Monnow, six and ten miles respectively from Monmouth, with White Castle on the hills above, guarding the important road over the pass to Abergavenny.

Whitecastle stands alone, but Skenfrith is an attractive village with an interesting church, and Grosmont, which was a borough until 1860, also has a handsome church, and many legends of Sion Kent (John of Kent) a local wizard reputed to have sold his soul to the devil 'whether buried inside the church or out'. He outwitted the Evil One by directing his neighbours to bury him beneath the church wall.

Gray, who spent many happy hours in the neighbourhood of Monmouth, having reached it by boat on his journey from Ross to Chepstow, says of its situation that it 'lies ... in a vale, that is the delight of my eyes, and the very seat of pleasure', and a mere glance at a map will show that it is a superb touring centre. Roads from Monmouth cross the Forest of Dean; others follow closely the course of the Monnow, and of the Trothy, which flows into the Wye south of Monmouth, and the A.466 rarely leaves the convolutions of the Wye on its way south to Chepstow. There is also an upper road (B.4293) through Trelleck (Tryleg), 600 feet above sea level, where some comparatively dull stretches are compensated for by magnificent views over the Wye and Usk Valleys.

At Redbrook, two miles below Monmouth, the river becomes the boundary between monmouthshire and Gloucestershire. St Briavel's castle, formerly the seat of the Constable of the Forest of Dean, high above the river, is now a Youth Hostel.

Llandogo, with its woods and little cascades, marks the tidal limit of the Wye, and on the next loop of the river is Tintern, with the ruins of its Cistercian Abbey beside the water, in a densely wooded valley which is no longer secluded in the tourist season.

Not even the largest numbers of chattering tourists can hide the soaring loveliness of the ruins, which are so impressive it is hard to believe the abbey could have been any finer in the period of its activity between 1131 and 1536. Those for whom the crowds are too great a distraction can view it in peace, even if more distantly, from the path through the woods on the left bank of the river. Poets have acclaimed it, and guide books abound; there can be no need to do more than urge a visit. Even the most hurried glimpse of the ruins leaves the memory of a beauty which can never fade.

Two miles below Tintern there is a footpath to the summit of Wyndcliff, a steep limestone mass rising nearly 800 feet above the river. It is another of the outstanding viewpoints of the Wye Valley, commanding the great loop of Lancaut, the estuary of the Severn, Steep Holm and Flat Holm, and parts of nine counties.

The road to Chepstow through St Arvans passes the entrance to the beautiful Piercefield Race Course, the most important in Wales, which inevitably involves delays on the days when there are races.

Chepstow, always a busy place, has become increasingly so since the opening of the Severn Bridge, although, mercifully, the M.4 by-passes the town on the south, and it has been able to preserve the gateway spanning the main road, part of the city walls, a noble parish church, and the enormous ramparts and great towers of the castle, which epitomize Marcher history and architecture. It is a magnificent ruin, whether seen from the river, or climbing up through the great wards from the entrance, or walking around the circuit of the ramparts.

Just as the castle buildings climb upwards from the roadway, so do the houses of Chepstow itself, for there is little level ground, and its steep, narrow, winding streets are at once a delight and a hazard to traffic. Much rebuilding has taken place, but there are some attrac-tive Regency houses. A gun displayed in Beaufort Square was given to Chepstow by George v to commemorate the award of the V.C. to William Charles Williams, a local sailor who was killed at Gallipoli.

Chepstow is particularly fortunate in having a very active local society which has published books on various aspects of local history, some of which give details of Chepstow's former importance as a port and shipbuilding centre. It was a trading centre for the river-borne traffic on the Wye and Severn, as well as for sea-going vessels, and a Customs Port until 1881. The Urban District Council still ranks as a Port Sanitary Authority, although it is now an agricultural, rather than a maritime centre, its trade having passed to Newport.

Since the opening of the Severn Bridge by H.M. The Queen in 1966, there is easy access from Chepstow to Bristol and Somerset.

The Offa's Dyke Path ends—or begins—at Sedbury Cliffs, over-looking the Severn on the English side of the Dyke, which can be reached from the A.48 to Lydney and Gloucester, but the supreme attraction, apart from the Wye Valley, is the Forest of Dean.

The Forest is one of the few surviving ancient Royal Forests of England, and was the first area in the country to be designated a Forest Park, under the care of the Forestry Commission. Isolated be-tween the tidal waters of the Severn and Wye, it remains a place apart, which has preserved its own pattern of life from time im-memorial. There are vast stretches of forest glades with giant oaks, ash-trees, hollies, birches and conifers, with many rare species of wild flowers and wild creatures of the forest.

The 22,000 acres covered by the Forest of Dean has practically the same boundaries as those fixed in 1668, although some areas of woodlands outside its boundaries have brought the area of the Forest Park to a total of 35,000 acres.

The Forest has been mined for iron ore since the time of the Romans, who had a large camp at Lydney, and among other Roman remains is a fine stretch of Roman road at Blackpool Bridge. Coal-mining has been carried on since at least the thirteenth century, and probably earlier. The Free Miners, who remain outside the national-ized industry, retain all their ancient customs, which were first re-corded in 1300. No one knows the origin of these rights, but the custom of a Free Miner swearing an oath with a stick of holly in his hand gave rise to a theory that they date back to the Roman occupa-tion, or even earlier. There is a brass in Newland church depicting a Forest Miner in fifteenth-century costume.

The Court of Verderers is one of the oldest institutions in England, and is said to have originated in the courts set up to administer the forest laws of King Canute.

In spite of the mining operations, the greater part of the Forest re-mains unspoiled, and each of its small towns and villages has some special attraction.

Innumerable books have been written about the Forest of Dean, and an excellent Forest Park Guide has been issued by H.M. Station-ery Office. Its status as a Forest Park has inevitably entailed the setting up of camping sites and 'Nature Trails', but these only touch a minute proportion of the whole—it is said there are over 2,000 miles of Forest paths, and there are still many places where a compass is advisable.

The ideal way to explore the Forest is, of course, on foot, but there are good roads, and in the days before the Severn Bridge was opened, when I left my Monmouthshire home for London by car, it was always by the Forest road from Monmouth to Gloucester and the Cotswolds, rather than by the Aust ferry, and it was always a memorable drive, at any time of the year.

The interlacing roads, which change their numbers (when they have any) over short stretches, make confusing reading until a good-scale map is consulted. There is such a choice of routes from Chep-stow to Monmouth or Ross that it is better for travellers to make a personal choice, although I cannot resist advising everyone to include the B.4226, which crosses the Forest from west to east, and passes the Speech House Hotel. The hotel is midway between Coleford and Cinderford. It was built in 1680 for the Court of the Verderers, and stands alone in the depth of the Forest, where it is possible to step across the road into woodland paths of almost unimaginable beauty and peace; a real refuge from the modern world.

CHAPTER ELEVEN

The Usk Valley

Breconshire (Sir Frycheiniog) lies between the purely agricultural county of Radnorshire and the densely populated mining valleys of Glamorgan and Monmouthshire. It is even more mountainous than Radnorshire, with over half between 1,000 and 3,000 feet above sea level. It covers the area which was once divided into Buallt, around Builth Wells in the north-west, which was part of Powys, and the kingdom of Brycheiniog, founded by the Irish Prince Brychan, who had married a Welsh princess. They had countless saintly children and grandchildren, to whom many of the Breconshire churches are dedicated.

The Brecon Beacons National Park (*Parc Cenedlaethol Bannau Brycheiniog*) covers an area of over 500 square miles, and is 45 miles wide, extending over the greater part of Breconshire eastward into Monmouthshire, to include the Black Mountains, and westwards into Carmarthenshire almost to Llandovery, and the Breconshire-Carmarthenshire Black Mountains, which are outside the scope of the Border country. There are a few main roads from north to south, but there is no road from west to east, apart from the A.40 along the northern border, from Llandovery to Brecon, where it turns south-east along the Usk Valley to Abergavenny. Few of the minor roads are practicable for cars, except in the south-east, and vast areas of the Park can be reached only on foot or on horseback, but some of the remotest places have tiny churches filled with treasures of woodwork, and there are countless viewpoints, comparatively few of which can be reached by motorists.

All the most attractive centres for exploring the part of the Park with which alone we are concerned here, are in the Usk Valley, or at Talgarth, Glasbury-on-Wye or Hay-on-Wye on the extreme north of the area. An excellent guide to the Park is published by H.M. Stationery Office.

Talgarth, a small market town between Hay and Brecon, on the western foothills of the Black Mountains, was once of great strategic importance, and there are the remains of a strong defensive tower, resembling a Northumbrian 'bastel-house', beside the bridge in the centre of the town. Talgarth also has an imposing church, with a strong defensive tower. A manuscript in the Bodleian Library gives the dedication '*Gwendolen aut Gwenfrewi*'; Theophilus Jones, commenting on this, says there can be no doubt about the true dedication: 'Gwenddolen, wife of Corineus, is the offspring of Titania, by Robin Goodfellow; Gwenfrewi was the eleventh daughter of Brychan, prince of Breconshire'.

Neuadd Felin, in Church Street, was the home of Jane Williams (Ysgafell) a nineteenth-century historian whose *History of Wales* was one of the best of the older histories of Wales. She also edited the *Autobiography of Elizabeth Davies* (or Cadwaladr), the Balaclava nurse who clashed with Florence Nightingale, and *The Literary Remains of the Rev. Thomas Price*, (*Carnhuanawc*), which are still the best sources of information on their respective subjects.

North-east of Talgarth is the round tower of Bronllys Castle, on a 400 ft. spur at the junction of the Dulas, Llynfi and Enig valleys, beside the road to Bronllys village. Freestanding round towers are a comparative rarity in most parts of the British Isles, but more than half the remaining examples are in South Wales, particularly in and around the county of Brecon. An eighteenth-century house has been built on to the thirteenth-century tower of Bronllys. There is a Norman church in the village, with a detached tower and part of a rood-screen.

Three churches within a radius of about four miles of Talgarth, although difficult of access, are well worth visiting, if only to compare their very different types of woodwork. Llaneleu, two miles east of Talgarth, has a primitive rood-screen with a tympanum carried up to the roof and decorated with white roses painted on a red background, and faint traces of a cross. The rough road from Talgarth can be negotiated by cars with care, but it must be approached on foot from any other direction, and the key must be fetched from the farmhouse opposite. The church is exactly 1,000 feet above sea level and commands breathtaking views of the Black Mountains.

Llandefalle, reached by a road with steep gradients from Bronllys, has a simple but well-carved open screen, without its rood-loft. It is reached by a narrow and very steep lane which passes a Victorian school and an eighteenth-century rectory. Llanfillo, reached by another poor road with steep gradients, along the valley of the Dulas, west of Talgarth, has a screen of about 1500, a perfectly restored rood-loft with unusual carvings, considerable Norman work, and other interesting features. The Rector, the Rev. Ifor Jones, has written an excellent guide, and I remember with pleasure the infectious enthusiasm with which he displayed his church to members of the Cambrian Archaeological Association on one of their annual outings.

Two roads run south from Talgarth to the Usk Valley, one along the valley of the Rhiangoll to Crickhowell, and the other through Trefecca to Llangorse and Bwlch.

Trefecca (Trefeca) was the birthplace of Howell Harris, the eighteenth-century religious reformer who was one of the 'Fathers' of Welsh Methodism. In 1752 he established a semi-monastic centre in Trefecca, which he financed and ruled extremely autocratically. When he died in 1773, he bequeathed all his possessions for the continuation of the community under the rules he had laid down, but in the course of time it changed its character and became a noted college for the education of Calvinistic Methodist ministers. It was closed in 1964, but there is an interesting museum in the chapel block, with exhibits from the Howell Harris community. Harris and his brother Joseph, who held an appointment in the Mint at the Tower of London, are buried in Talgarth church.

Until a few years ago, Llangorse Lake (Llyn Safaddan), was a reed-bordered stretch of water with scarcely a house in sight, visited only by a few anglers and boating enthusiasts who found its calm and peaceful beauty very soothing, but it has been invaded by speed boats, and has an Adventure Centre and numerous caravan and camping parks!

There are numerous legends of a submerged city in the lake which are probably folk-memories of prehistoric lake dwellings, for about

1925 a '*cafn unpren*' (a primitive canoe made out of a single tree-trunk) was found there. Giraldus Cambrensis also tells that the birds of the lake bore testimony by their song that Gruffydd ap Rhys was the rightful owner of the land, and not the Norman lord who claimed it.

Bwlch, just beyond the point where the B.4560 joins the A.40, has traces of a Roman fort. It is associated with the sinister saying 'Once through the Bwlch (pass or gap) a Welshman never returns', which was probably all too well justified during the stormy centuries of Border warfare.

Although the River Usk (Afon Wysg) flows through the grandest mountain regions of South Wales, it has never had the fame of the Wye Valley. It is considerably shorter; does not flow through great gorges or make the extraordinary horseshoe bends of the Wye, and is only navigable to Crichowell, less than half the distance navigable on the Wye, yet two poets greater than any the Wye has produced drew their inspiration from its idyllic scenery—Henry Vaughan and W. H. Davies.

A string of attractive little towns with their mingling of historic interest and cultural and sporting activities has produced an admirably diverse range of 'worthies', and its salmon and trout fishing have drawn tributes from many devoted anglers, although perhaps none so surprising as Sir Harry Lauder's comment after a fishing holiday there: 'I'd like to know where there's a bonnier valley and bonnier water than the Usk for fishing'. High praise indeed from such a patriotic Scot, who was acquainted with the superb fishing in his native country!

Brecon (Aberhonddu), the county town of Breconshire, is roughly in the centre of the northern border of the Brecon Beacons National Park. It is set where the Honddu and the Tarell join the Usk, with the Brecon Beacons rising on the south to a height of nearly 3,000 feet. Its streets are so erratically planned that newcomers are apt to lose their way, but with so many surviving Georgian houses it has a dignity all its own. Christ Church College, one of the two public schools of Wales, incorporates a thirteenth-century monastic church, and the noble Priory Church is worthy of its status as the cathedral of the bishopric of Swansea and Brecon created in 1923.

Among the many walks in the neighbourhood is one along the old Roman road to Y Gaer, three miles west of Brecon, where the remains of the Roman fort, which was occupied by the Vettonian Spanish Cavalry, can be seen. Finds made when the site was excavated by Sir Mortimer Wheeler are now in the Country Museum at Brecon.

Two roads run south-east along the valley of the Usk to Crickhowell. The B.4558, south of the river, is pleasant enough, but most people will choose the A.40, on the north of the river, which keeps fairly close to the Usk, through the scenery which Henry Vaughan loved so well, and where his finest poetry was written, as he recalls in The Water-fall:

> *'Dear stream! dear bank, where often I*
> *Have sate, and pleas'd my pensive eye ...'*

Henry Vaughan, 'The Silurist', as he called himself, adapting the name from the Silures who once inhabited the region, and also known as 'The Swan of Usk', was kinsman to the Vaughans of Tretower and the Herberts, and cousin of John Aubrey of *Brief Lives* fame. He alone of the seventeenth-century mystical poets was completely bi-lingual, and even claimed Welsh as his mother tongue. He lived the greater part of his life in the parish of Llansantffraid (Llansanffraid). Newton (Trenewydd) where he was born, is now a farmhouse which may incorporate fragments of his birthplace, and the cottage to which he retired as an elderly widower has been demolished, although the sturdy walls of the old Tower farmhouse below Scethrog to which it was attached remain. He spent some years in Brecon as Clerk to Sir Marmaduke Lloyd, Chief Justice of the Brecon Circuit, but the busy streets had little appeal for him and he wrote some amusing and witty verses on the town. He escaped whenever he could to the beautiful Priory Groves 'His usual Retyrement', which still enhance the surroundings of Brecon Priory, and where he met his future wife. He seems to have lived for all his married life at Newton, and is buried at his express wish in the churchyard of Llansantffraed, and not in the church as was then customary for the gentry. He lies under a large, flat stone with an inscription composed by himself. Members of the Brecknock Society visit it annually, and after hearing a commemorative sermon, lay a wreath on the grave.

More fortunate than his contemporary, Traherne, he was read in his own day, and his poems have been republished many times, notably the beautiful edition edited by Ernest Rhys for the Gregynog Press and adorned with woodcuts by Robert Ashwin Maynard and Horace Walter Bray. Several biographies, and a novel have also appeared.

Beyond Llansantffraed the A.40 deserts the Usk to skirt the northern foot of Craig Llwyd Fawr and Myarth through Bwlch, where there are fine views up and down the valley, to Crickhowell (Crucywel), which climbs a steep hill above a splendid seventeenth-century bridge of 13 arches, which links it with Llangattock (Llangatwg) on the opposite bank of the Usk. The church is set so high that although its broach spire is not very tall, it can be seen for miles. Crickhowell Castle, which figures frequently in accounts of thirteenth-century wars, was ruinous when Leland visited it, and there is now only the motte and bailey, parts of the curtain wall and a small round tower. The earlier Norman castle may have been on a roadside mount a mile to the north-west, and there was an Iron Age camp on Crucywel (Table Mountain). There is a massive gatehouse on the north-west, which is all that remains of the Tudor house of the Herbert family.

Crickhowell is sheltered on the north by Pen Cerrig-calch, a peak over 2,000 feet high, which has a calcareous cap, and is the only outlier north of the Usk of the mountain limestone whose great crags dominate Crickhowell from the south. South of the river, steep and difficult roads lead to Craig y Ciliau on the north of Mynydd Llangattock, and Cwm Clydach, on the south-east, near Brynmawr, two of the Nature reserves of the Park which require special permission before they can be visited.

Half a mile north-west of Crickhowell, and high above the main road is Gwernvale, the birthplace in 1790 of Sir George Everest, the Surveyor-General of India, after whom Mount Everest was named. In 1906, Frederick Rolfe ('Baron Corvo') spent many weeks there as the guest of the Pirie-Gordon family, until he showed himself in his true colours and the hospitable house closed its doors to him.

Two miles farther along the road to Talgarth, in the long and beautiful Rhiangoll Valley, is Tretower (Tretŵr) Court, the most perfect and beautiful example of a medieval manor house in Wales, and not to be surpassed in England. It has been meticulously restored by the Department of the Environment, largely through the efforts of Sir John Lloyd and the Brecknock Society. Sixteen generations of the Vaughan family held Tretower, until it was sold in 1783. Begun in the fourteenth century, it was added to up to 1630, and is walled, with a gatehouse worthy of a medieval castle. Nearby is a Norman castle built by the Picards, to whom the lordship of Ystrad Yw was given by Bernard Neufmarché, Lord of Brecon. Built to control the southern end of the pass from the Usk to the Wye, it was originally a rectangular keep on a stone-faced motte. In the thirteenth century, a round keep was built inside the stump of the older tower, and turrets were built around the bailey. It was finally abandoned when Tretower Court was built.

Farther up the valley is Cwm Du, or, more correctly, Llanfihangel Cwm Du, of which the Rev. Thomas Price (Carnhuanawc) was Vicar from 1825 until his death in 1848. He was one of the most learned and attractive figures of nineteenth century Wales. During the time he attended Brecon Grammar School, he became friendly with Theophilus Jones, and drew the illustrations for the second volume of his *History of Brecknockshire*. Carnhuanawc worked untiringly to promote the cause of the Welsh language and literature. He also promoted the Breton language, and helped in the translation of the New Testament into Breton by Le Gonidec.

East of Crickhowell are the Grwyne Fawr and Grwyne Fechan valleys, which penetrate the heart of the Black Mountains. They meet at Llanbedr, which has a Perpendicular church, and some attractive houses in the neighbourhood. The combined rivers flow south through Llangenny, with a sixteenth century church and Tudor farmhouses, to join the Usk.

The road up the Grwyne Fechan degenerates into a footpath, but the road up the Grwyne Fawr, through oak woods in the lower reaches, and thick plantations of larch and spruce higher up the valley, continues across the border into Monmouthshire, and eventually winds south to Abergavenny. It is also possible to reach the

valley of the Honddu above Llanfihangel Crucorney (Crucornau) by a road which strikes off from Fforest. Near Fforest is the Pont-yr-Esgob (Bishop's Bridge) over the Grwyne Fawr at the point where the river is turned westward by a fault line. It commemorates Archbishop Baldwin, who crossed it in the company of Giraldus Cambrensis in 1188.

A little beyond the Pont Newydd (New Bridge) there is an unsignposted track climbing steeply to Patrishow church, for which the key must be obtained at the Tudor farmhouse beside the stony path. Even by Welsh standards, it is difficult to find Patrishow, but it was this difficulty of access which preserved it from iconoclasts, and it is well worth the trouble of seeking it. It is often approached from Abergavenny, although access is no easier from there, but it is interesting to visit it after seeing the three small churches around Talgarth, already mentioned, for its great richness of carving completes the series of contrasts of these Breconshire churches.

There is something about these remote churches in all parts of Wales, so small, and so simple on the outside and so glorious within, that is infinitely moving, and none more so than at Patrishow. The medieval church has three pre-Reformation altar-tables, a font with an inscription believed to refer to Genyllian Foel, Prince of Powys in the eleventh century; a curious little thirteenth-century cell; murals which include a figure of Death, with an hour-glass, scythe and accompanying skeleton; an oak cradle roof; and, most splendid of all, a Welsh-type Tudor rood-screen, with magnificently carved vines issuing from the mouth of a Welsh dragon. There are far-reaching views from the church.

The six miles from Crickhowell to Abergavenny run between the Blorenge and Mynydd Llangattock on the south, and the Black Mountains, with the distinctive Sugar Loaf mountain, in the north. The road crosses the Grwyne near its confluence with the Usk, and continues over the county boundary into Monmouthshire.

Although these mountains reach a height of under 3,000 feet, and can look deceptively friendly on bright summer days, they rise so abruptly that they have all the majesty of far greater heights. On stormy days, the Black Mountains well deserve their name, towering menacingly above the valleys, and especially intimidating

30 *The River Wye at Chepstow; the castle and Rennie's iron road bridge*

when seen from the English plain. They are mainly of Old Red Sandstone, but there are great crags where the alternate layers of sandstone and shale make them impossible for even the most experienced rock climbers.

Abergavenny (Y Fenni), an ancient market town set where the little Gavenny River joins the Usk, and ringed with mountains, has always been a place of strategic importance, where the entry to the Usk Valley and to Bwlch, the gateway to Central Wales, could be closed at will by its lords. The Romans had their fortress of Gobannium there, which may lie below the ruined medieval castle, whose motte and bailey, and fourteenth-century gatehouse, are within a park on the south-west of the town. There is also a museum which owes much to the enthusiasm of Abergavenny's historian, Mr Alfred Jackson, who has written an excellent guide to the town and castle.

It was in this castle that William de Braose perpetrated the most notorious of his many foul deeds by inviting 70 Welsh guests to a feast, and murdering them all—a breach of hospitality which shocked the Welsh nearly as much as the deed itself. It is strange to find Giraldus Cambrensis, who was harsh enough in condemning the gluttony of the monks he hated, condoning the ill-doing of William de Braose, apparently because, like so many of the Normans, he was generous to the Church, and prefaced all his acts with the formula 'In the name of God ...'. De Braose managed to survive for some 30 years, until he quarrelled with King John. He then, with typical meanness, escaped to France, leaving his wife, Maud de St Valery, and his son, to bear the brunt of King John's wrath. As she refused to give up her son as hostage to the man 'who had murdered his own nephew' (Arthur of Brittany), he had her and the boy walled up alive —by some accounts, at Corfe Castle, and by others, at Windsor.

There are some Tudor and Georgian houses in the town, but the glory of Abergavenny is its Priory Church, almost all that survives of the Benedictine Priory. There is some Norman work, but the greater part dates from the fourteenth century. There are fine canopied choir stalls with misericords, with a mitre distinguishing the Prior's seat. The oldest effigy in the church is only 4 ft 6 ins in length, and has been identified as Eva de Braose, daughter of William Marshall, Earl of Pembroke, and wife of the eighth lord of Abergavenny, but is more probably Lady Margaret Plantagenet, wife of John Hastings, Earl of Pembroke. It was recorded in the sixteenth century that her left hand held the image of a squirrel, now lost, and there is a tradition that she overbalanced and fell from the castle battlements to her death, in trying to catch a pet squirrel which had escaped.

Another effigy may represent Eva de Cantalupe, or her daughter Joan who married Henry Hastings, first Lord Hastings, who died in 1268. The effigy has a shield charged with three large fleurs-de-lis, believed to be the only example of a female figure bearing a knightly shield on her body. Among the Herbert and Hastings tombs is the wooden effigy of a young knight in armour. It is probably that of John, second Lord Hastings and Baron Bergavenny, who died in 1313, or his son, the third Lord Hastings, who died in 1325. The effigy is so beautifully and spiritedly carved that it is surely a portrait.

A magnificent figure of Jesse, once part of a Jesse tree, is possibly the most perfect surviving, and is unique in being carved out of a single piece of wood, ten feet long. An excellent guide gives detailed particulars of the monuments, the eighteenth century mural tablets, and the old brasses with their curious epitaphs.

As an exceedingly busy and important market centre, and a point of departure for the Brecon Beacons National Park, Abergavenny's streets are usually crowded, but its most glittering occasions were in the mid-nineteenth century, when it was the centre of the Welsh Literary Revival. Under the joint planning of the Rev. Thomas Price (Carnhuanawc), Lady Hall (Gwenynen Gwent, afterwards Lady Llanover), and Lady Greenly of Titley Court, the Cymdeithas Cymreigyddion y Fenni (Abergavenny Welsh Literary Society), founded in 1833, in the little Sun Inn, drew many distinguished visitors. Among others were Ambassadors from several European countries, Henry Hallam, the historian, Professor Carl Lepsius, Professor Schultz, Dr Charles Meyer, Alexis François Rio, the Comte Theodore Hersart de la Villamarqué, and Dwarkanauth Tagore, the great grandfather of Rabindranath Tagore, the poet and mystic.

An annual eisteddfod, followed by dinner at the Angel, was held for 21 years, reviving interest in the Welsh language and culture through much practical work, at a time when English had almost swamped the Welsh language. It was largely due to the Abergavenny

Society that others sprang up all over Wales, and that the Welsh language survived at all.

Eleven miles north-west of Abergavenny is the valley of the Honddu, a romantic prelude to Llanthony Priory, which is included in the Brecon Beacons National Park.

Founded in the twelfth century as an Augustinian monastery, the remains are of Norman, Early English and Transitional work, the Chapter House, Slype, Prior's Lodge and south-west tower being partly incorporated in a hotel. There is a fine columbarium, and a parish church of very early date which was probably the hospitium of the monks until the Dissolution. Llanthony was the Mother house of the Gloucestershire Llanthony, by which it was superseded in importance.

The estate was bought by Walter Savage Landor in 1807. He built a new house, since demolished, but quarrelled with the country folk, and finally left the estate in the hands of trustees. Four miles farther up the valley is the new Llanthony Abbey, founded for Benedictine monks in 1870 by Father Ignatius (the Rev. Joseph Leycester Lyne), member of a well-known Monmouthshire family. There is an account of the building, and of Father Ignatius and his parents, in Kilvert's *Diary*. Soon after his death and burial in the church in 1908, the community ceased to exist, and the buildings fell into ruin. In 1924, Eric Gill, the sculptor, went to Capel-y-ffin, at the head of the valley, with his family, and was joined there for a year or two by the eminent artist, David Jones.

Roads run north-east from Abergavenny to Hereford and the Three Castles, and the A.40 continues to Raglan and Monmouth. The A.4042 runs south down the Usk Valley to Llanover, from which Sir Benjamin Hall took his title when he was raised to the peerage in 1859. 'Big Ben', the bell which is now famous as the B.B.C. time signal, was named after Sir Benjamin, who was 6 ft 7 ins in height, and as First Commissioner of Works, was instrumental in arranging for the bell to be cast. Sir Benjamin was also responsible for great reforms in the local Government of London. Henry Jepson, says in *The Sanitary Evolution of London* that Hall's Act for the better Local Management of the Metropolis, passed in 1855, was 'the turning point in the sanitary history and evolution of London', and the *Official*

History of the London County Council says: 'This Act was the most important single measure passed for the government of London, and for the first time introduced an ordered system ...'. Yet this, and other good work he did in his 26 years in Parliament—most of them representing the London borough of St Marylebone—are now forgotten.

Lord Llanover and his wife were friends and correspondents of Queen Sophie of Holland, the first wife of King Wilhelm III, and entertained her at their London house when she was in England. Her eldest son, the Prince of Orange, stayed with them at Llanover in 1860. Baron de Bunsen, who had married Lady Llanover's eldest sister, Fanny, brought many distinguished diplomats to stay at Llanover, but always it was a centre of Welsh culture, and the mainstay of the 'Llanover Circle' were Welsh men and women who all worked tirelessly in the cause of the Welsh Literary Revival. Lord Llanover also fought in Parliament for the Welsh language, protesting against the continual appointment of clergymen who could not speak the language of their parishioners. The Welsh Church he and Lady Llanover established on his estate at Abercarn, some 10 miles to the south-west in the valley of the Ebbw, above the wooded Nant Gwyddon, still holds its services in Welsh.

Lady Llanover was a redoubtable champion of the 'Monmouthshire is Welsh' party. The question only arose after the great influx of English people following the Industrial Revolution, for Monmouthshire's history and traditions were all Welsh. Most of its place-names bear witness to its Welsh origin as the Kingdom of Gwent and today it is within a Welsh diocese, and comes under Welsh authorities for education, sport, electricity, gas, and all other purposes. The supporters of the claim that Monmouthshire is English base their claim chiefly on the fact that under the Act of Union the county was included in the Oxford Circuit, and as Lady Llanover so trenchantly said, the argument is so fallacious that on this basis it would be equally possible (and ridiculous) to claim that Chester is Welsh because it is included in the North Wales circuit!

South of Llanover, at Little Mill, the A.472 branches off on the right to Usk (Brynbuga), now a peaceful little place, which has had a stormy history of fierce fighting. Set where the foothills of the

Black Mountains begin, its castle is on a precipitous rock above the market square and the river. The walls follow the contours of the hill, and the ruins include two square towers and a round tower, and portions of the great hall.

It is believed Roman *Burrium* was on this site, but it first rose to importance in Norman times, when its powerful lords included the de Clares and Mortimers. It was here Henry, Prince of Wales, the future victor of Agincourt, won his first great military success in 1403, when he relieved the hard-pressed garrison, and inflicted a crushing defeat on the Welsh forces commanded by Owain Glyn Dŵr's son, Gruffydd.

All that remains of the priory founded by Richard de Clare early in the twelfth century is the gatehouse, now the entrance to a private garden, and the spacious church, which is partly Norman, with a north aisle added in the fifteenth century, and two porches about a century later. The Perpendicular screen has a small brass bearing the earliest known example of an inscription in the Welsh language on a brass. It is believed to be a panegyric on a local lawyer, Adam of Usk, who played a leading part in the deposition of Richard II, and chronicled English history from 1377 to 1421.

Another native of Usk was Arthur Russell Wallace, whose manuscript on the origin of species, sent to Darwin in 1858, outlined a theory similar to Darwin's own. A joint exposition was read to the Linnean Society, and Darwin gave full acknowledgement to Wallace's ideas in his own writings.

That most delightful of companions, Archdeacon Coxe, whose *Historical Tour Through Monmouthshire* was published in 1801, speaks of the manufacture of Japan ware at Usk. This industry was begun at Pontypool in the late seventeenth century by the Allgood family, who also set up a branch at Usk, which was in production until the middle of the nineteenth century. The process involved lacquering on iron plates, and was a closely guarded secret. Specimens of Pontypool and Usk Japan ware are now highly prized by collectors.

Usk has a famous inn, The Three Salmons, and a fine old bridge across the Usk, and it is a centre for a region of fascinating small villages, and for Raglan, half-way between Usk and Monmouth.

Raglan is a pretty little village with a magnificent castle, which differs from all the other castles of Gwent in owing its splendour entirely to the family pride of owners who only attained importance in the fifteenth century. It had little strategic importance, and formed no part of the original Norman plan for holding down the newly conquered, but far from quiescent Welsh. It probably originated in the fourteenth century as a small defensive manor house which came to the Herberts, and later by marriage to Charles Somerset, first Earl of Worcester, an ancestor of the Dukes of Beaufort.

The Somersets, whose story is told in *The Somerset Sequence* by Horatia Durant, were devoted adherents of Charles I, and poured out their wealth in his cause. Although Raglan had been developed as a splendid Tudor palace, it withstood a protracted siege in the Civil War, captained by the first Marquess of Worcester, then aged about 85. The garrison finally marched out with all the honours of war, but the aged marquis was thrown into prison. The only concession made was that he should be buried at Windsor, upon which the gallant old man exclaimed 'God bless my soul, they will give me a grander castle when dead, than they took from me when living'. The extensive ruins are now in the care of the Department of the Environment.

Below Usk is Newbridge, and Kemeys Inferior, a seat of the Kemeys family, whose mansion is now a farm. The Folly on the hill above was built in 1712, in a Roman encampment, by George Kemeys, the last male of his line, who told his uncle: 'I can see eleven counties from it', to which his uncle retorted: 'Then eleven counties can see thy folly'.

The Usk flows from Kemeys through level meadows to Caerleon (Caerllion), a quiet and pleasant but undistinguished village whose colourful and romantic memories are centred on the Roman remains of Isca, part of which lie beneath the later buildings. Much, however, has been recovered by excavations carried out under Sir (then Dr) Mortimer Wheeler, Aileen Fox, Christopher Hawkes and, above all, by V. E. Nash-Williams. Sir Mortimer, who began the excavations in 1926, tells in his autobiography *Still Digging* of that realization of every archaeologists' dream—a telephone call offering instant and adequate financial backing. As a result the splendid Roman amphitheatre was exposed to view, at a cost to the sponsors, *The Daily Mail*, of several thousands of pounds. Later excavations enabled the general plan of the fortress and details of the social life of the inhabitants to be traced.

The amphitheatre is now in the care of the Department of the Environment.

There are innumerable books about Caerleon, for whether King Arthur and his Knights of the Round Table gathered there or not, there is magic in the very name of Caerleon, which will always be an inspiration to scholars, archaeologists and poets. Even the neighbouring Caerwent (*Venta Silurum*), the only civilian town of Roman Wales, has not quite the same appeal, although massive stretches of the Roman wall survive, and its lay-out and history are described in the guide issued by the Department of the Environment.

It is easy to understand why Arthur Machen, who has written so delightfully about the neighbourhood, believed that the inspiration for his stories came from his good fortune in being born in Caerleon, and spending his childhood there.

Below Caerleon the Usk has little attraction now-a-days. Its muddy banks are only hidden at high tide, and the 'villages so green' of which W. H. Davies writes have now almost disappeared under housing estates and the gigantic steel works of Llanwern. Only Magor still clusters around its great church, in the meadows beneath the hills of Wentwood.

Busy, bustling Newport, 'new' only because the Norman port superseded Roman Caerleon, can no longer show the birthplace of W. H. Davies, but still has its Norman castle beside the Usk; its ancient parish church, now the cathedral of St Woolos; the Westgate Hotel which was the centre of the Chartist Riots in 1839; and its wonderful 'Double View' at Allt-yr-yn. It has become an even more convenient touring centre since the opening of the Severn Bridge.

The M.4 runs just north of Newport, but there is a more peaceful road (A.48) past Penhow (Pen-hw) castle and Caerwent to Crick, where it joins the M.4 a few miles west of the Severn Bridge. No more appropriate place could be found from which to take leave of the Border Country than Isca, the most southerly fort along the Roman Road from Deva from which we started.

Index

The numerals in **bold** type refer to the figure numbers of the illustrations

Abbey Dore, 170, 171, 172; **19**
Abel, John, 150, 166, 171, 183
Abercarn, 205
Aberedw, 174-175
Abergavenny (Y Fenni), 192, 198, 201, 202-204
Aconbury, 180
Acton Burnell, 119, 124, 125
Adam of Usk, 206
AEthelflaed, 34, 97
Alfred, King, 34
Alleluia Victory, 58-59
All Stretton, 100, 101, 103, 104
Almeley, 166
Alun, Valley of the, 54-58, 64, 69
Ape Vale, 122-123
Archenfield (Erging), 169
Arrow, River, 134, 142, 151, 152, 153, 162
Arthur, King, 17, 136, 186, 208
Ashford Bowdler, 148
Ashford Carbonel, 148
Asterton, 101, 102-103, 114
Aston-on-Clun, 126
Aymestrey, 143

Bacton, 172
Baldwin, Stanley, first Lord, 120
    Thomas, 120
Bangor-on-Dee (Bangor Iscoed), 70
Bankes family, 40
Barnston, Roger, 70
Berrington Hall, 149
Basingwerk, 18, 41, 42-43, 58, 69
Baystonhill, 99
Beguildy, 132
Berriew, 90
Berwyn Mountains, 30, 31, 76, 77, 79-80, 81
Betws-y-Crwyn, 131-132
'Big Ben', 166, 204

Bishop's Castle, 111, 112-113, 126, 131
Black Mountains, 170, 177, 179, 192, 194, 198, 201-202; **28**
Blackwell, Rev. John (Alun), 61
Bleddfa, 137
Bleddyn ap Cynfyn, 19
Bodfari, 52-53
Bodrhyddan Hall, 47, 65
Borrow, George, 28, 76, 77, 80, 141
Boydell, John, 37
Brampton Bryan, 134-135
Braose, William de, 175, 177, 202
Brecon (Aberhonddu), 26, 167, 192, 193, 195-196, 198
    Beacons National Park (Parc Cenedlaethol Bannau Brecheiniog), 30, 192-204
Bredwardine, 172, 178
Breidden Hills, 86-87
Bridge Sollers, 168, 177
Brimfield, 147, 148
Britten, Benjamin, *Noyes Fludde*, 35
Bromfield, 107, 134
Bronllys, 193, 194
Brynbella, 46, 52
Bryn Iorcyn, 65-66
Buckley, 61-62
Buildwas, 42
Builth Wells (Llanfair-ym-Muallt), 174, 192
Bull, Dr John, 159
Bulmer, H. P., 162
Burney, Dr Charles, 85
Buttington, 87-88
Bwlch, 195, 197, 202
Byron, Lord, 142

Caer Caradoc, 100-101
Caergwrle, 64, 65, 66
Caerleon (Caerllion), 16, 17, 207-208
Caerwent (Venta Silurum) 208

Caerwys, 28, 45, 53-54, 65
Cain Valley, 79, 81
Canon Pyon, 162, 165
Capel-y-ffin, 204
Caradog (Caractacus), 16, 86, 101, 135, 140
Cardiff, 46, 157
Carr, Rev. Edmund Donald, 101-102
Castle Caereinion, 89
Ceiriog, River, 20, 76, 77
Chepstow, 24, 184, 188-189, 190; **30**
Chester, 16, 18, 28, 31, 32-36, 41, 61, 62 68, 69, 70, 83, 106
    Cathedral, 33; **2**
    Earls of, 19, 25, 36, 64
    Nativity Plays, 34-35
    Rows, 32
    Port of, 34, 35
Chirbury, 95, 96-97
Chirk (Y Waun), 16, 67, 76
    Castle Gates, 76; **8**
Chomondeley, Mary, 99
Church Stretton, 15, 100, 101, 102, 103, 104, 123
Cider, 161-162, 180
Cilcain, 58
Clifford family, 120, 177
Clifford-on-Wye, 24, 177
Clun, 24, 78, 106, 112, 125, 126-130, 131, 132
    Forest, 31, 130-133, 137
Clunbury, 126, 130
Clungenford, 125, 130
Clunton, 126, 130
Clwyd, Vale of, 36, 46, 47, 48, 50, 52, 76
Clwydian Hills, 45, 46, 52, 53, 58, 59, 62
Clive, Robert, first Lord, 83, 88, 114
Clyro, 130, 175, 176
Cockshutt, 72
Coke, Frances, 129, 133
Condover, 99
Corve Valley, 119-120, 121
Courtfield, 185-186
Cox, David, 161
Cradoc, Rev. Walter, 68
Craven Arms, 31, 106, 126, 135
Credenhill, 161, 162, 168
Crickhowell (Crucywel), 194, 195, 196, 197; **26**
Croft Castle, 144
Cwm, 45, 46
Cwm Du, see Llanfihangel Cwm Du

Cynddelw Brydydd Mawr, quoted, 59

Dafydd ab Edmund, 53, 71
Dafydd ap Llewelyn, 23
Dafydd Ddu Athro o Hiraddug, 50
Darwin, Charles, 84, 206
Davies, Gwendoline and Margaret, 94, 95
    Sir Henry Walford, 79, 94
    John, 160-161
    John Scarlett, 161
    Robert and John, 63, 68, 76; Iron-work by; **7, 8**
    W. H., 195, 208
Dean, Forest of, 30, 186, 188, 189-191
Dee, River, 15, 31, 33, 35, 36, 41, 43, 45, 52, 69, 70, 76, 77
Deerfold Forest, 144
Defoe, Daniel, quoted, 48, 124, 150
Dic of Aberdaron (Richard Robert Jones), 48
Dickens, Charles, 33, 83, 103, 183
Diddlebury, 120
Dilwyn, 165
Donne, John, 96
Dore Valley, see Golden Valley
Dorstone, 170, 173
Downing, 44
Downton, 144
Doyle, Sir Arthur Conan, 142
Dunstable, John, 159
Dyserth (Diserth), 45-46, 47, 50, 52

Eardisland, 152; **17**
Eardisley, 166-167
Easthope, 123
Eaton Bishop, 179
Eisteddfod (Caerwys), 28, 45, 53-54
    Royal National, 54, 75
Elgar, Sir Edward, 153, 160
Elias, John, 47
Ellesmere, 71-72
Ellis, Rev. Robert (Cynddelw), 77
Evans, David, 93
    Grace, 89
    Mary Ann (George Eliot), 40
Everest, Sir George, 197
Ewloe Castle, 39-40
Ewyas, 169, 170
    Harold, 24, 170-171
Eye Manor, 149
Eyewood, 142

Farndon, 69

Index

Faulkner, Thomas, 114
Feddw Circle, 138
Felton, Rev. William, 159
Fferm, 63
Ffrith, Y, 65
Fitzosbern, Robert, see Hereford, Earls
  of
Flint (Fflint), 39, 40, 65
Forden Gaer, 89
Forest Inn, 138, 139
Fownhope, 156, 179
Fuller, Thomas, quoted, 32, 160-1

Gam, Sir David, 27
Garreg Hill, 44
Garrick, David, 160
Gaulle, General de, 72
Geoffrey of Monmouth, 17, 186, 187
Gerard, John, quoted, 161-2
George, David Lloyd, first Earl Dwyfor,
  60
Gill, Eric, 204
Giraldus Cambrensis (Gerallt Cymru),
  26, 42, 47, 48, 78, 133, 138-9, 171, 195,
  202
Gladlas Hall, 72
Gladstone, William Ewart, 36-39
Glan-yr-Afon, 44, 45
Glasbury-on-Wye (Y Clas-ar-Wy), 175,
  192
Glyn Dŵr, Owain, 23-24, 27, 31, 71, 78,
  80, 96, 138, 139, 172, 178, 206
Glynceiriog, 76, 77, 79
Glynne, Catherine, 36
  Lord Chief Justice John, 36
Godiva, Lady, 34, 121, 151
Golden Valley, 169, 170-173
Goodrich, 184-185
Goodwin, Geraint, 93
Gorsedd, 43
Gray, Thomas, 187; The Triumphs of
  Owen, 20
Greenly, Lady, 142, 203
Griffiths, Ann, 81
Griffiths, Dennis, 62
Gregynog Hall, 94-95;
  Press, 94-95, 197
Gresford, 42, 68-69
Grosmont, 187
Gruffydd ab yr Ynad Coch, quoted, 23
Gruffydd ap Cynan, 20, 53
Grwyne Fawr, 198, 201
  Fechan, 198

Guilsfield, 90
Guinevere, Queen, 17, 136
Guy, Thomas, 183
Gwaenysgor, 45
Gwalchmai, 20
Gwenwynwyn, 23, 88
Gwernvale, 197
Gwyn, St Richard, 68
Gwyn, Nell, 160
Gwysaney, 58, 62

Habberley, 108
Hakluyt, Richard, 151
Halkyn (Helygain), 40, 41, 58
Hall, Benjamin, see Llanover, Lord
Hall-of-the-Forest, 133
Hanmer, 53, 71; 5
Harraden, Beatrice, 104
Harris, Howell, 194
  Joseph, 194
Hart, Emma, Lady Hamilton, 39, 87
Hartsheath Hall (Plas yn Hersedd), 63-64
Harvest Festival Services, 50
Hawarden (Penarlag), 35, 36-39, 59
Hay-on-Wye (Y Gelli), 167, 173, 175, 176-
  177, 192, 193
Heath Church, 120
Herbert family, 88, 89, 172, 196, 197,
  203, 207
  Edward, Lord, 96
  George, 96
Hereford, 28, 143, 147, 149, 154, 155-161,
  162, 166, 167, 168, 169, 177, 179, 185,
  204; 20
  Bishops of, 113, 149, 156, 157, 159, 167
  Cathedral, 156-157, 158, 159, 160
  Chained Libraries, 155, 156, 158-159
  Earls of, 19, 24, 157
  Three Choirs Festival, 155, 159, 160
Herefordshire School of sculpture, 143,
  170
Hergest, 141, 153-154
Hemans, Mrs Felicia, 48
Henry IV, 31, 41
Henry V, 27, 185, 186, 187, 206
Henry VII, 28, 40, 45, 82, 143
Hickman, Dr Henry, 107
Holme Lacy, 179, 180, 183
Holmes, Sherlock, 142, 184
Holt, 69
Holywell (Treffynnon), 39, 41-42, 43
Honddu, River, 177, 195, 201, 204
Hope, Shropshire, 112

Index

Hope, Flintshire, 64, 65
Hopesay, 126
Hopkins, Gerard Manley, 51-52, 96
Hopton Castle, 125
Housman, A. E., 118-119, 125, 130
   Laurence, 119
Howard, Sir Robert, 129, 133
Hunt, Dame Agnes, 79
Hunt, Lord, 18
Hugh Lupus, Earl of Chester, 25, 34, 36
Hughes, John Ceiriog (Ceiriog), 77
Hughley, 119, 123

Ignatius, Father (Rev. Joseph Leycester
   Lyne), 204
Ippikins Rock, 123

Jefferson, Thomas, 77
John ap John, 68
Johnson, Dr Samuel, 45, 46, 48, 50, 162
Jones, David, 204
   Sir Robert, 47, 79

Kemble family, 33, 160
Kerry (Ceri) 133
   Hills, 130, 132
Kenchester, 156, 168
Kerne Bridge, 185
Kemeys Inferior, 207
Kilpeck, 143, 167, 169-170, 178; **23**
Kilvert, Rev. Francis, 176, 178, 204
Kingsland, 152
Kingsley, Charles, 41, 43, 54
   Henry, 104
King's Pyon, 162-165
Kington, 134, 137, 139, 141, 151, 152-154,
   167
Kinnersley, 166
Kinnerton, 139
Kinsham Court, 142
Knighton (Trefyclawdd), 18, 112, 126,
   132, 134, 135, 137, 139
Knucklas, 19, 135-136
Kynaston, Humphrey, 102
Kyrle, John, 183
   Sir John, **13**
   Sibyl, **14**
Lacy family, 24, 25, 116, 167, 170
Landor, Walter Savage, 204
Langley, near Acton Burnell, 119, 124
Langley, Corve Dale, 119
Lauder, Sir Harry, 195
Lea Stone, 114

Ledbury, 162
Lee, Samuel, 100
Leebotwood, 100
Leeswood Hall (Coed-llai), 63; White
   Gates, **7**
Leete, The, 54-57, 58
Leighton, Lord, 104
   Lord Chief Justice, 125
Leintwardine, 134
Leofric, Earl, 34, 121, 151
Leominster, 143, 147, 149-151, 154
Lewis, Eiluned, 93
Lewis Glyn Cothi, 32, 153
Limebrook Priory, 144
Lingen, 144
Linley Hall, 112
Little Stretton, 104, 105
Llananno, 136
Llanasa, 45
Llanbedr, Breconshire, 198
Llanbedr-Painscastle (Llanbedr Castell-
   paen), 175
Llanbister, 136
Llandefalle, 194
Llandegly (Llandeglau), 137-138
Llandogo, 188
Llaneleu, 193
Llanelwedd, 174
Llanerch, 50, 65
Llanfair Caereinion, 81, 89, 90
Llanfihangel Crucorney (Crucornau),
   201
Llanfihangel Cwm Du, 198
Llanfihangel Nant Melan, 138
Llanfihangel Rhydiethon, 137
Llanfihangel-yng-Ngwynfa, 81
Llanfillo, 194
Llanfyllin, 81
Llangattock (Llangatwg), 197
Llangenny, 198
Llangollen, 16, 42, 72-76
Llangorse Lake (Llyn Safaddan), 194-195
Llangunllo, 136
Llangynidr, 31
Llangynog, 79
Llanllwchaiarn, 93
Llanrhaeadr-ym-Mochnant, 28, 80
Llansanffraid Glynceiriog, 77, 93
Llansansantffraid Newton, 196
Llanthony Priory, 26, 204; **1**
Llanover, 142, 166, 204-205; **27**
   Lord and Lady, 166, 203, 204-205
Llanvair Waterdine, 132

Index

Llanwnog rood-loft, **9**
Llowes, 175, 176
Lloyd, David, 44
  John Ambrose, 61
  Rev. John, 54
Llwyd, Angharad, 54
  Morgan, 68
Llys Edwin, 40
Llywelyn ap Gruffydd, 23, 26, 36, 53, 94
  ab Iorwerth, 23, 59, 78, 129
Loggerheads, 58
Long Mynd, 100, 101-103, 115
Longnor, 99-100
Longtown, 170
Ludford, 147-148
Ludlow, 15, 24, 93, 98, 106, 107, 115, 116-118, 122, 125, 132, 134, 144, 147; **12**
Lugg, River, 134, 136, 137, 139, 140, 142, 144, 147, 152, 154
Lybury North, 114
Lydham, 112
Lydney, 189, 190
Lyth Hill, 98, 99

Mabinogion, The, 20, 87, 154
Machen, Arthur, 208
Maclaren, Ian (Rev. John Watson), 104
Madog ap Maredudd, 20
Madley, 169, 171, 179
Maelor Saesneg (English Maelor), 70-71
Maen Achwyfan, 44
Maesyronen Chapel, 175-176
Mainstone, 131, 133
Mathews, Charles James, 63-64; *Jennie Jones*, 63
Meifod, 79, 81, 93
Meliden, 46
Mendelssohn, Felix Bartholdy, *The Rivulet (Fantasias, Op. 16)*, 54, 57
Meole Brace, 98
Meyrick, Sir Samuel Rush, 185
Middleton on the Hill, 149
Milton, John, *Masque of Comus*, quoted, 117
Minton, 101, 102
Moccas, 178
Moel Fammau, 52
Moel Hiraddug, 45
Moeran, E. J., 153
Mold (Yr Wyddgrug), 52, 58, 59-61, 62, 70
Molesworth, Mrs, 118

Monaughty, 137, 139
Monmouth (Trefynwy), 24, 27, 184, 186-187, 188, 190, 204, 206; **29**
Monnington Court, 172
  Straddel, 172, 178
  -on-Wye, 172, 177-178
Monnow River (Afon Mynwy), 157, 169, 170, 177, 186, 187, 188
Montgomery (Trefaldwyn), 24, 95-96
  Roger of, 24-25, 96, 121, 126
More, 112
Morfa Rhuddlan, 47
Morgan, Bishop, 28, 48, 80
Mortimer family, 24, 27, 135, 139, 140, 143, 152, 206
Mortimer's Cross, 143, 144
Morys, Huw, 77, 80
Mostyn, 45
Much Birch, 180
Much Marcle, 180; **13, 14**
Much Wenlock, 121-122, 123
Munslow, 118, 120
Myddle, 72, 102
Myndtown, 101, 102
Mytton family, 108, 121
  Jack, 108

Nannerch, 54
National Trust, 77, 88, 123, 126, 144, 149
Nelson, Admiral Lord, 187
  Museum, 187
Nercwys, 62
Newcastle, Salop, 131, 132, 133
Newland, 190
Newport (Cas Newydd), 31, 106, 186, 189, 208
New Radnor, 138-139, 140, 167
Newtown (Trefnewydd), 29, 89, 90-93, 94, 95, 105, 132, 133, 136
Nightingale, Florence, 142, 193
Northop (Llaneurgain), 40

Offa, King, 18, 84, 113, 140, 153, 157
Offa's Dyke, 18, 19, 36, 41, 52, 65, 88, 97, 130, 131, 133, 135, 140, 152, 177, 189
Oldcastle, Sir John, 144
Old Radnor, 139
Orleton, Herefordshire, 148-149
  Adam de, 148-149
Oswestry, 18, 25, 76, 77-79, 87
Ouseley, Rev. Sir Frederick, 159
Overton-on-Dee, 42, 65, 70, 71
Owain Cyfeiliog, 20, 90

Index

Owain Gwynedd, 20, 59
Owen, Daniel, 60-61
  Robert, 89, 90-93
  Wilfred, 79
Pantasaph, 43
Parr, Old, 87
Parry, Blanche, 172
  John (Bardd Alaw), *Cader Idris*, 63
  William, 40
Patrishow Church, 201; **24, 25**
Pembridge, 151-152
Pennant Melangell, 80
Pennant Abbot Thomas ap Dafydd, 43, 44
  Thomas, 40, 44, 54, 62
Pennsylvania, 53, 68
Pentre Hobyn, 62-63
Pen-y-Bont, 137
Peterchurch, 172
Pilleth, 139,
Piozzi, Mrs 46, 50, 52
Pistyll Rhaeadr, 42, 80
Pitchford Hall, 124
Plaish, 125
Plas Teg, 64, 69
Plowden Hall, 114; **4**
Pontesbury, 98, 107, 108
Pontesford, 107, 108
Pope, Alexander, 148, 183
Powell, Vavasour, 93, 136
Powis Castle (Castell Coch), 16, 88-89
Prestatyn, 18, 46
Presteigne (Llanandras), 134, 139, 140-142
Price, Rev. Thomas (Carnhuanawc), 154, 193, 198, 203

Radnor Forest, 134, 136-139, 142
Raglan, 204, 206, 207
Ratlinghope, 101, 103
Reid, Capt. Mayne, 184
Rhayader (Rhaeadr Gwy), 137, 174
Rhual, 58
Rhuddlan, 25, 47; **3**
  Statute of, 19, 47, 65
Rhydspence, 174, 177
Rhyd-y-Mwyn, 54
Rhyl, 46-47, 54
Richard II, 34, 41
Richard's Castle, 140, 144-147, 170
Roberts, Rev. John, 51
Rodd, The, 142
Rolfe, Frederick (Baron Corvo), 42, 197
Rolls, Hon. Charles Stewart, 187

Rossett, 69
Ross-on-Wye, 180, 183-184
Rowland, Daniel, 160
Rowton Moor, Battle of, 34
Ruabon, 16, 72; **6**
St Asaph (Llanelwy), 45, 48-49, 50, 59, 133
St Beuno's College, 51-52
St Briavel's, 188
St Cyndeyrn, 48
St David (Dewi Dyfrwr), 89, 169
St David's, diocese of, 26, 133
St Dyfrig (Dubririus), 169
St Werburg, 34
St Winifred (Glenfrewi), 41, 42
Saltney, 35
Sarnesfield, 165-166
Say family, 24, 78, 106, 126-129
Scott, Sir Walter, 16; *The Betrothed*, 23, 129, 175
Scudamore family, 171, 172, 179-180, 183
Sedbury Cliffs, 18, 189
Seven Wonders of Wales, The, 41-42, 67, 69, 71
Severn, River (Afon Hafren), 18, 29, 79, 82, 86, 87, 90, 93, 94, 123, 133, 157, 189
  Bridge, 188, 189, 190, 208
Shelley, Percy Bysshe, 142
Shelve, 108, 112
Shipton Hall, 121
Shobdon, 142-143; **21**
Shrewsbury, 24, 28, 70, 72, 76, 82-86, 93, 98, 99, 100, 107, 111, 121; **10**
  Abbey, 81
  Cakes, 85-86
  Museums, 83
  School, 84
Shropshire Union Canal, 71, 77, 90
Siddons, Mrs, 33
Sidney, Sir Henry, 84, 116-117
  Sir Philip, 84, 116
Skenfrith, 187
Smith, Miles, 161
Soughton Hall, 40
Speech House, 191
Spring, Tom (Tom Winter), 156
Stained Glass, 51, 69, 93, 98
Stanley, Sir Henry Morton (John Rowland), 48-49
Stanner Rocks, 139
Stanton Lacy, 119
Stapleton, 99

Staunton-on-Arrow, 152
Stiperstones, 101, 111-112, 114
Stokesay Castle, 106-107; **11**
Strata Marcella, see Ystrad Marchell
Stretton, Hesba (Sarah Smith), 103-104
Symonds Yat, 186; **22**

Talgarth, 94, 192, 193, 198, 201
Tanat Valley, 79, 80
Tarlton, Richard, 99
Teme, River, 107, 132, 134, 135, 147, 148
Thompson, Francis, 43
Thrale, Mrs, see Piozzi, Mrs
Three Castles (The Trilateral), 187, 204
Tintern, 184, 188
Titley Court, 142, 203
Tower, 62
Traherne, Thomas, 161, 168-169, 197
Trefecca (Trefeca), 194
Trelawnyd (Newmarket), 45
Trelleck (Tryleg), 188
Trelogan, 44, 45
Tremeirchion, 50-51, 52
Tretower Court (Tretŵr), 27, 172, 196
  198
Trevalyn Hall, 69
Tyberton, 178, 179

Usk (Brynbuga), 205-206, 207
  River (Afon Wysg), 15, 142, 192-208;
  26, 27

Valery, Maud de St., 175, 176, 177, 202
Vaughan family, 27, 141, 153, 172, 178,
  185-186, 196, 198
  Henry (The Silurist), 168, 195, 196-197
Vowchurch, 172
Vyrnwy, Lake, 81
  River, 20, 79

Walcot Hall, 114
Wales, National Library of, 45, 54, 73
  Museum of, 46, 61, 65, 73, 95
Wallace, Alfred Russell, 160, 206
Walton, 139-140

Water-Break-Its-Neck, 138
Wat's Dyke, 18, 40, 41, 42, 72, 78, 152
Weatherley, Fred, 160
Webb, Mary, 98-99
Welshpool (Trallwm), 86, 88, 89, 90, 93,
  95
Wenlock Edge, 31, 119, 120-121, 122, 125
Wentnor, 101, 102-103
Weobley, 165; **16**
Weston-under-Penyard, 184
Weyman, Stanley, 118
Wheeler, River (Afon Chwiler), 50, 52,
  53, 54
Whitcott Keysett, 133
White Castle, 187
Whitford (Chwitfordd), 43-44
Wigmore, 24, 126, 140, 143, 144
Wilderhope Manor, 122, 123
Williams, Emlyn, 44
  Henry (Ysgafell), 93-94
  Jane (Ysgafell), 94, 193
Wilson, Richard, 58, 60, 63, 95
Wilton Castle, 180-183
Wistanstow, 105-106, 115
Wordsworth, 140, 142, 153, 185
Woolstaston, 101, 102, 115
Worthenbury, 71
Wrekin, The, 101, 121
Wrexham, 16, 42, 62, 63, 66, 67-68, 69,
  70, 72
Wycherley, William, 84
Wye, River (Afon Wysg), 15, 136, 155,
  157, 168, 169, 171, 173, 174-191, 195,
  198; **15, 18, 20, 22, 30**
Wyndcliff, 188
Wynne, Dr Thomas, 53
Wynnstay, 68, 72

Yale, Elihu, 67, 78
  University of, 67, 148
Yapp, Sir Arthur Keysall, 149
Ystrad Marchell (Strata Marcella), 20, 89,
  90

Index